TABLE OF CONTENTS

LIST OF FIGURES

LIST OF TABLES

LIST OF ACRONYMS AND ABBREVIATIONS

FBI	Federal Bureau of Investigation
CIA	Central Intelligence Agency
DOD	Department of Defense
OSD	Office of the Secretary of Defense
PLA	People's Liberation Army
PLAN	People's Liberation Army Navy

ACKNOWLEDGMENTS

This work would not have been completed without the guidance and encouragement of the Defense Analysis department staff and fellow students at the Naval Postgraduate School. Our advisor, Dr. Hy Rothstein, and second reader, Dr. Kalev I. Sepp, were patient portraits of calm, even when we switched topics in our fourth quarter to focus on China's aircraft carrier instead of counter-piracy in the Horn of Africa. Despite our late start, they guided us unnervingly to a sweet finish with their incisive inputs and encouragement. Dr. Lee Doo Wan and Captain Roberto Dulzaides also picked our brains and gave us a great deal of advice for our work. My thesis partner Kuei-Lin's contributions in gathering and interpreting sources for our research have been invaluable, and I apologize for the material that he gathered that we did not include inside here. His wife, Ya-Ting, has also supported us wholeheartedly. Our families have become wonderful friends for life. Most importantly, my wife, Cindy Goh, has been a pillar of strength, a river of sustenance and an indefatigable aide-de-camp at home to ensure our world didn't fall apart as I mugged and labored through endless nights of typing. It has been a breathless and unforgettable journey of learning and thought

—Kong Eu Yen

I would like to express my appreciation to all those who provided me the support to complete this thesis. I give a special thanks to our thesis advisor, Professor Hy Rothstein, whose contribution in suggestions and encouragement helped us construct our thesis concepts. I would also like to acknowledge with much appreciation the crucial role played by Professor Kalev I. Sepp, who gave us the initial inspiration for this thesis in his class on deception. The most important person I give my deepest appreciation to is my thesis partner, Kong Eu Yen, for helping me to conquer language barriers, for stimulating discussions, for the sleepless nights we worked together and for the fun we shared during the past 18 months. Finally, I am forever grateful to my wife, Wen Ya-Ting. Her quiet patience, encouragement, and unwavering love were the critical foundations to my schooling at the Naval Postgraduate School.

—Yu Kuei-Lin.

I. INTRODUCTION

A.   BACKGROUND OF THE STUDY

On 25 September 2012, the *Liaoning* "辽宁" was commissioned into the People's Liberation Army Navy (PLAN) as the People's Republic of China's first aircraft carrier. From a military capability perspective, the carrier was notable for its understatement—it was built from a 1980s era Soviet legacy design and it wasn't the first modern carrier in the East Asia region.[1] It had yet to integrate its organic aircraft onboard and even the Chinese government downplayed the carrier's military significance, stating that it was meant for "scientific research and military training".[2]

However, from a public relations perspective, the *Liaoning*'s commissioning was a major news event that generated international and regional interest far greater than the carrier's ostensible military capabilities. The symbolic significance of China's first aircraft carrier and the strategic implications of this military development were the unspoken elephants in the room (or on the pier) that sunny day on 25 September 2012 in the naval port of Dalian—the cradle of the PLAN. It was also not lost on the media that the timing of the *Liaoning*'s commissioning preceded the 63rd anniversary of the founding of the People's Republic of China on 1 October 2012. Both President Hu Jintao and Premier Wen Jiabao, were in attendance at the *Liaoning*'s commissioning, further underlining the symbolic significance of the event.[3]

A notable reference from China's state media coverage of *Liaoning*'s commissioning is the relatively innocuous reference to *Liaoning*'s launch after "years of refitting and sea-trials."[4] For informed observers, "re-fitting and sea trials" is poor cover for the storied transformation of the *Liaoning* from a rusting, disemboweled ex-Soviet

---

[1] Japan's Hyuga-class light carriers (2009), India's INS *Viraat* (1987) and Thailand's HTMS *Chakri Naruebet* (1996) preceded the *Liaoning* in the Western Pacific region.

[2] "China's first aircraft carrier commissioned," *Xinhua* (China), 25 September 2012, http://news.xinhuanet.com/english/china/2012-09/25/c_131871538.htm.

[3] "Chinese President attends aircraft carrier '*Liaoning*' handover ceremony in Dalian," *Xinhua* (China), 25 September 2012, http://news.xinhuanet.com/english/photo/2012-09/25/c_131872638.htm.

[4] "Chinese President attends aircraft carrier '*Liaoning*' handover ceremony in Dalian," *Xinhua.*

hulk into the pride of the PLA Navy and the military embodiment of China's rise to great power status. The staid reference also obscures the successful employment of deception by China to protect the development of her first aircraft carrier with Churchill's famed "bodyguard of lies." This study aims to demystify and decipher China's strategic deception regarding the *Liaoning* and provide insights into how the fast rising political and military heavyweight of the East handles strategy and employs deception. Henceforth, reference to China's deception stratagem relating to the *Liaoning* shall be referred to as the *Liaoning* deception in this work.

B.   PURPOSE OF THE STUDY

This thesis studies the acquisition and development of *Liaoning* from a strategic perspective and seeks to understand how China employed deception to protect the birth of its first aircraft carrier. To improve understanding, this study lays out the significant phases of the *Liaoning* Deception and details how China managed the deception ploy from inception to fruition. It studies the main factors driving the *Liaoning* deception— China's national and military strategies. The *Liaoning* deception is also analyzed for its veracity and effectiveness. Finally, the study looks at how the *Liaoning* deception informs us about China's intentions for the role of the aircraft carrier *Liaoning* in the future.

C.   ORGANIZATION OF THE STUDY

The methodology of this thesis and the rationale for selecting the *Liaoning* as a study case are explained in Chapter II. This thesis begins by equipping the reader with an understanding of China's maritime strategy and national strategic goals to make sense of China's desire for an aircraft carrier. The concept of deception is introduced to the reader with a specific focus on Chinese strategic deception to allow for comprehension about the nature and method of Chinese strategic deception. The theory of analysis of competing hypotheses by intelligence scholar Richards J. Heuer will be used to analyze the *Liaoning* deception and make assessments about the competing hypotheses regarding the

2

Liaoning's role and purpose.[5]   China's aircraft carrier program exhibits several characteristics that make it a suitable case study for understanding how China employs strategic deception in the development of its military capabilities. Among other reasons, the huge signature of an aircraft carrier makes it extremely difficult to hide and the nature of its capabilities is easy to estimate. These immutable characteristics only elevate the importance of deception in protecting the actual intent of this military capability.

Chapter III begins by examining China's strategic psyche and national security goals. These provide us with a macro-perspective on the drivers behind Chinese strategic thinking and their formulation of national security goals. It lays the foundation for the deeper examination of maritime strategy and strategic deception in the later chapters.

Chapter IV lays out China's maritime strategy based on contemporary evidence examined in other studies. Examining maritime strategy and goals would facilitate understanding how the aircraft carrier capability would be of utility in achieving those goals. Understanding China's maritime strategy will improve our ability to analyze the *Liaoning* deception—why it was necessary, what its intent was and whether it has yet unfulfilled objectives.

Chapter V examines deception as a military stratagem to facilitate understanding its employment in various guises in contemporary Chinese strategy. This study will also highlight the differences between Western and Eastern concepts of deception. By Western, the authors refer to the Western European and American understanding of deception, along the lines espoused by Daniel and Herbig in *Strategic Military Deception*.[6] Western understanding of deception perceives it as a separate branch of strategy that is executed in the shadows and burdened with a sinister reputation of dishonesty and deceit.[7] This contrasts with the Eastern tradition that views deception as an inseparable part of strategic calculus and the perfect execution of which is not only a

---

[5] Richards J. Heuer, *Psychology of Intelligence Analysis* (Central Intelligence Agency: Centre for Study of Intelligence, 1999), 102.

[6] Donald C. Daniel and Katherine L. Herbig, *Strategic Military Deception* (New York: Pergamon, 1982), xii.

[7] Scott A. Boorman, "Deception in Chinese Strategy" in *The Military and Political Power in China in the 1970s*, ed. William W. Whitson, 313-328 (New York: Praeger, 1972).

matter of pride but a means to avoid conflict altogether. The Chinese understanding of deception is alluded to in historical Chinese works like Sun Tzu's *Art of War* and examined in Sawyer's *The Tao of Deception*.[8] Deception in China has long historical tradition and is exemplified by the vernacular terms and stories linked to deception as a concept. The Thirty-Six Stratagems that are popular in Chinese cultural and literary traditions provide a convenient way to gain insight into the psyche of Chinese deception.[9] Their wide range of applicability facilitates the employment of distinct deception methods. This chapter explains how relevant elements of the Thirty-Six Stratagems can be used to interpret the *Liaoning* Deception. Understanding the difference between Eastern and Western conceptions of deception will allow a more nuanced understanding of deception as employed by the Chinese. Thus, Chapter V focuses on deception as a military strategic concept and the Chinese understanding and application of deception in particular.

Chapter VI studies the acquisition and development of the *Liaoning* in detail, tracing it from inception to early 2013. The *Liaoning* Deception could have been conceptualized with the intent of hiding the true purpose of the acquisition of a disemboweled, rusted and incomplete hulk from Ukraine. After unveiling the carrier to the world, the *Liaoning* Deception could involve masking the true operational roles of the aircraft carrier and downplaying its capabilities. These possibilities are explored to gain a better understanding of how China hides the growth and development of an important and extremely visible capability using stratagem.

Having gained an understanding of the *Liaoning* Deception, competing hypotheses pertaining to the purpose of the *Liaoning* will be examined in Chapter VII. The objective of the analysis is the falsification of alternate hypotheses based on evidence gathered and the assessment of the true role of the *Liaoning*. The first hypothesis proposes that the *Liaoning* is intended for training and research purposes and will not

---

[8] Ralph D. Sawyer, *The Tao of Deception* (Cambridge, Massachusetts: Basic Books, 2007), 1.

[9] Haichen Sun, *The Wiles of War* (Beijing: Foreign Language Press, 1993). The 36 Stratagems are individually explained in the *The Wiles of War* and are studied as part of the Chinese language in Chinese elementary school as well as in the Chinese military.

lead maritime operations for the PLAN. The second hypothesis proposes that the *Liaoning* is not merely intended for training and research, and will be an operational platform of note in the PLA Navy's order of battle. It will also form the cornerstone around which China will build a major capability based on aircraft carriers. The third hypothesis proposes that the *Liaoning* is but a poorly conceived naval project that will fail to achieve its training and research, and operational goals. The theory of competing hypotheses will be applied and relevant evidence available until early 2013 will be analyzed.

The last chapter will compile the implications of this study for China, the East Asia region and the U.S. It will also suggest lessons learned from the *Liaoning* Deception case to facilitate a deeper understanding of China's future strategic moves.

D. LIMITATIONS OF THE STUDY

This study examines China's aircraft carrier program and how deception supports China's strategic goals. This will be achieved through an understanding of China's strategic goals, maritime strategy, deception ploys and deception management. This study does not intend to make critical assessments of China's aircraft carrier from engineering, financial or doctrinal perspectives.

Although an understanding of China's maritime strategy is necessary for understanding China's deception strategy, this study does not critique China's maritime strategy. The study is focused on China's aircraft carrier capability and its management of interested parties' perceptions about the aircraft carrier. China's maritime strategy will be examined only to provide a strategic background to understanding China's intent for the aircraft carrier *Liaoning*.

E. CHINESE LANGUAGE CONVENTIONS USED

As this thesis makes frequent reference to Chinese language sources, names and terms, it is important to note the type of convention used by the authors for the romanization of Chinese words and the type of Chinese script used for Chinese characters in this work.

5

For romanization of Chinese, this work uses the Pinyin convention which is the standard for the U.S. and Chinese governments, United Nations and most media organizations. The Library of Congress's guidelines for the Pinyin standard will be adopted for this work.[10] This departs from the older Wade-Giles system of romanization which was in widespread use until the 1980s. An example would be the name of the Chinese communist leader Mao Tse-Tung. Wade-Giles convention romanizes his name as "Mao Tse-Tung". The Pinyin convention romanizes his name as "Mao Zedong". The Chinese characters for his name are "毛泽东".

When non-Pinyin references are more widely known, they are retained for ease of comprehension. An example would be the strategist Sun Tzu. Wade-Giles convention romanizes his name as "Sun Tzu". Pinyin convention romanizes his name as "Sunzi". The Chinese characters for his name are "孙子". To facilitate cross-referencing, works that utilize the older Wade-Giles convention will still be referenced using that system. All other Chinese references in this work will be romanized under the Pinyin convention.

For Chinese characters in this work, simplified Chinese script will be used. The Chinese script is divided into the traditional and simplified scripts. Simplified Chinese script was instituted by China's leader Mao Zedong in the 1950s as part of efforts to simplify Chinese script and increase literacy in China—it involves the reduction in the number and complexity of Chinese characters. Today, traditional Chinese script is used in Taiwan, Hong Kong and much of the Chinese diaspora. Simplified Chinese script is used in China, Malaysia and Singapore. The debate over the merits of simplification and preservation of traditional Chinese script is an ongoing issue. The choice of simplified Chinese script in this work is to facilitate study by a non-Chinese audience who is likely to have been schooled in simplified Chinese. Whenever feasible, initial references to Chinese names and sources will be followed by their Chinese characters.

---

[10] Phillip Melzer, "Library of Congress Pinyin Conversion Project: New Chinese Romanization Guidelines," Library of Congress, 3 November 1998, http://www.loc.gov/catdir/pinyin/romcover.html.

II. METHODOLOGY AND CASE STUDY SELECTION

A. INTRODUCTION

This chapter explains the methodology behind this thesis, its organization and case study selection. The purpose of this thesis is to decipher China's employment of strategic deception in the acquisition and development of its first aircraft carrier—the *Liaoning*. This study draws on both ancient and contemporary history to study China's deception as the authors believe that Chinese strategic psyche is heavily influenced by its own perception of history and China's place in the larger constellation of global civilizations. The secretive nature of deception also means it is best studied ex post so that it can be studied retrospectively on the basis of known events and actions. Ultimately, this thesis strives to improve understanding of China, its strategic culture, its use of strategic deception and hopefully inform future engagements with this fast rising Eastern power.

The linkages between the critical elements involved in the *Liaoning* deception are laid out in Figure 1 on the following page. The three elements that directly impacted the *Liaoning* deception are China's national strategic psyche, its tradition of employing deception, and its military goals and strategy. This thesis proposes that the nature and motivation of China's national and military strategies drove the need for an aircraft carrier —while its cultural propensity for deception drove the employment of strategic deception to safeguard the *Liaoning*'s development.

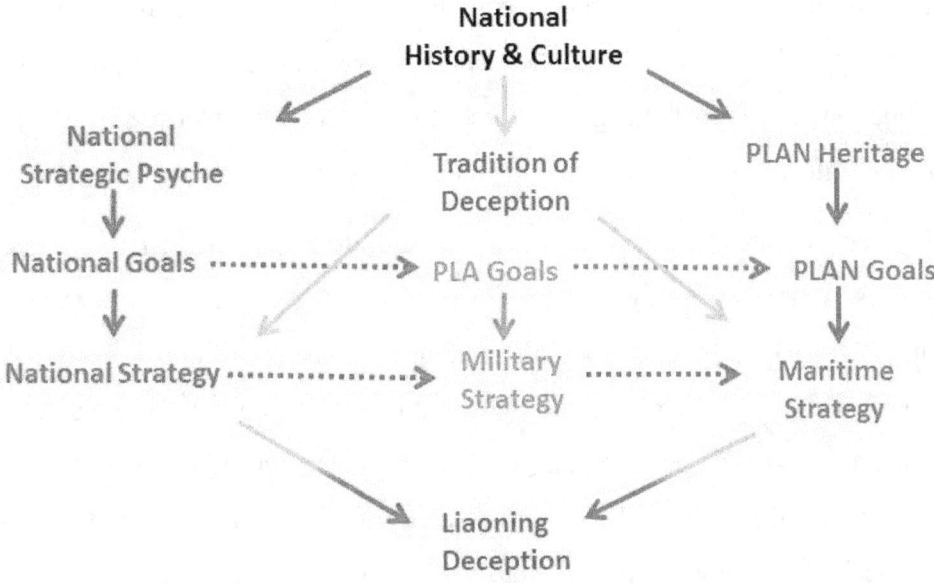

Figure 1.   Relationship of Elements of *Liaoning* Deception

B.   HYPOTHESIS

This thesis proposes that the acquisition and development of China's first aircraft carrier *Liaoning* was a deliberate strategic deception ploy that was driven by China's national and military interests. The veracity of this hypothesis will be examined in this thesis by an examination of the environment (history, culture), structures (state, military) and strategy (national, maritime, deception); as well as a detailed examination of the evolution of the *Liaoning*'s acquisition and development. The questions that this thesis will answer: Was the acquisition and development of the *Liaoning* a deception? What were its motivations? How was it executed? What are the implications of the *Liaoning* deception?

C.   ANALYSIS

The hypothesis will be analyzed in two parts. This first part will be a three pronged look at China's national goals and strategy; its military goals and strategy; and its deception goals and strategy. These three levels of analysis are complimentary and inter-related as each preceding level directly influences the next level below. This analysis explains how policy goals at the national and military levels drive the formulation of strategy and how those strategies lead to the development of an aircraft carrier capability. The goals of deception and China's strategy of employing deception are then applied to the national goal of acquiring a carrier. Combined, they form a coherent and mutually reinforcing strategic deception strategy.

The second part of analysis investigates the intricacies of the *Liaoning* deception. This involves a detailed study of the critical events and timeline of the *Liaoning* deception. It also highlights China's publicly stated positions regarding carrier development in the lead up to the *Liaoning*'s commissioning. The disparity between word and deed will be investigated and assessment made on the evidence and possible reasons for such a disparity. The theory of analysis of competing hypotheses will be applied to the *Liaoning* case for greater clarity about the *Liaoning*'s future role.

D.   ASSUMPTIONS

The approach taken by this thesis makes the following assumptions about the entities being analyzed. While there may be evidence to the contrary of the assumptions made, the authors felt that these assumptions were reasonable and would serve more good than harm in facilitating analysis of the *Liaoning* case.

With regard to the Chinese government, its military and the People's Liberation Army Navy, the assumption was made that these were unitary actors at their respective levels. This meant that leadership and policy guidance flowed through their respective chains of command and were heeded and executed. This thesis does not account for rogue actors acting on their own —independent of national policy goals and objectives.

It was also assumed that the entities of interest in this thesis were rational actors that acted in accordance with their respective interests at the organizational and national levels. This assumption is critical because the basis of our argument about the motivations behind strategic deception is driven by national self-interest.

The final assumption is that contemporary Chinese strategic culture is influenced by China's civilizational history and its various political and thought leaders through time.[11] This thesis does not conduct any empirical test of the relationship between strategic culture and history. Rather, it accepts that linkage and makes associations between the two. The thesis provides many instances where anecdotal evidence suggesting a linkage between the two is discussed.

E. KEY APPROACHES

1. Centrality of Chinese National Culture and History

To study Chinese strategic deception, our approach first pursued an understanding of the broader historical and cultural background that influenced all three critical elements of our thesis - Chinese strategic psyche, Chinese tradition of deception and the People's Liberation Army Navy's (PLAN) heritage. The reasons for the importance and broad influence of history and culture in China are myriad and explained only briefly within the scope of this work. However, a few critical reasons bear identification:

- Chinese history has been quite meticulously recorded and is easily accessible to the population through traditional and modern media. Many of the old methods of passing down stories through theatre and literature are now supplemented by websites, videogames and movies. New generations are exposed to it not just in school but society at large.

- Chinese history is actively studied in a society that still places great emphasis on education. The nature of the Chinese language, with its rich verbal tradition and unified written script rooted in history and culture, makes learning it as a language as much a study of history as it is linguistics.

- The Chinese people are fond of their civilizational history. Although this is hardly limited to the Chinese since any people tracing their civilizational roots to a rich history are no less justified in feeling a sense of deep pride, few civilization have been as introspective and inward looking as China. While other civilizations have tended to expand outward, the Chinese were content to build up their Middle Kingdom and consolidate their civilization with minimal outward expansion. Central to this tendency was the perception that the Middle Kingdom was the center of civilization and all else that revolved around it was inferior. [12]

---

[11] Alastair Iain Johnston, *Cultural Realism* (New Jersey: Princeton University Press, 1994), 22.

[12] Henry Kissinger, *On China* (New York: Penguin Press, 2011), 10.

The influence of history and culture on many facets of Chinese national life has therefore been significant. Even while the present Chinese generation builds upon the present for the future, the present in also influenced and guided by its past. Chapter III on China's Strategic Psyche and Chapter IV on China's Maritime Heritage and Strategy explain how they directly impact on China's deployment of the *Liaoning* deception.

### 2.	China's Strategic Psyche

In studying China's strategic psyche in Chapter III, the thesis examined facets of China's history relevant to the formulation of strategy and assessed to be key characteristics of China's strategic thinking. Four key features were assessed to be of significance to the study of strategic deception involving the *Liaoning*. While these features were by no means exclusive to China, their combination and the depth of their influence on China's strategic psyche was assessed to be significant.

### 3.	China's Goals and Strategies

Policy documents published by China's government and policy statements from China's leaders were the primary sources for the identification of China's national goals. The relevance of those goals was compared with the state of national development in China and its national priorities. An overarching national strategy predicated on "China's peaceful development" was identified from a 2011 White Paper from China.[13] The thesis probed deeper into national security goals in the maritime arena as this was the primary area of interest relevant to China's aircraft carrier capability. Policy statements from China's Defence White Papers were studied for insights into China's maritime policy goals.

### 4.	China's Maritime Strategy

Believing in the salience of China's history on its contemporary developments, China's heritage in the strategic maritime arena was studied. It illustrated the strategic irrelevance of maritime capabilities in China's predominantly land-warfare dominated history. The rising importance of the PLAN from the late 20th century was studied

---

[13] *China's Peaceful Development*, Information Office of the State Council of the People's Republic of China, 6 September 2011, http://www.china.org.cn/government/whitepaper/node_7126562.htm.

11

through an examination of its increasing relevance to China's national strategy and its improving capabilities. With the PLAN's increasing prominence in national security, the appointment of Liu Huaqing as PLAN Commander was highlighted as he represented an important milestone in the modernization of the PLAN and the genesis of China's maritime strategy. Known as the father of China's aircraft carrier program, Liu's pivotal role in influencing the PLAN's carrier capability was examined.[14]

5. China's Strategic Deception

China's employment of strategic deception with regard to its aircraft carrier development was examined through the influence of three lines of inquiry. The first was China's propensity to employ strategic deception in peace to achieve its strategic goals. The second was the influence of Chinese leader Deng Xiaoping's hide and bide strategy. The third was the influence of elements of the Thirty-Six Stratagems that advocated various means in which to employ deception.

F.   SELECTION OF CASE STUDY

The case of the *Liaoning* was selected as it satisfied the following criteria that not only facilitated research but made her a compelling case for the study of strategic deception:

- The *Liaoning* represented a significant strategic capability for China as its first aircraft carrier, thus there was significant academic and professional interest in her genesis.

- As a significant national capability, the *Liaoning* served as a useful test case because its genesis was a result of deliberation about national and maritime goals and strategy. Study of the *Liaoning* deception not only provides insight into deception at the strategic level but also improves understanding about China's maritime ambitions.

- Material concerning the *Liaoning* was both abundant and accessible, thus making the research effort manageable.

---

[14] Nan Li and Christopher Weuve, "China's Aircraft Carrier Ambitions: An Update," *Naval War College* Review, Winter 2010, Vol. 63, No.1: 13-31, last accessed 2 June 2013, http://www.usnwc.edu/getattachment/99679d4b-cbc1-4291-933e-a520ea231565/China-s-Aircraft-Carrier-Ambitions--An-Update.

- There was significant evidence that the acquisition and development of the *Liaoning* was shrouded in purposeful deceptions about her true purpose.

- The development of the *Liaoning* is but one of many significant developments made by China in the area of engineering, science and technology with military applications in the first decade of the new millennium. As a significant military and naval capability, the *Liaoning* therefore serves as a useful platform to integrate developments in other areas.

G. EXAMINATION OF THE CASE STUDY

The *Liaoning* case study is first examined through a chronological study of the events that transpired in the acquisition and development of the aircraft carrier and associated capabilities. This initial investigation seeks to highlight the discrepancies between China's statements and known developments of the *Liaoning*. The second phase of analysis proposes a plausible deception ploy that was employed in the *Liaoning* deception. This is the triple-layered cover story that the authors believe was central to the deception ploy involving the *Liaoning*. The final phase of analysis proposes various measures employed by China to manage the *Liaoning* deception until it achieved its final purpose.

H. POSTULATING ABOUT THE *LIAONING*'S TRUE ROLE

The last analytical chapter employs Richards Heuer's analysis of competing hypotheses to postulate the *Liaoning*'s true role in the PLAN and as part of China's maritime strategy. [15] It will investigate three competing hypotheses:

1. The *Liaoning* is intended for training purposes and does not signal China's interest in building a major capability based on aircraft carriers.

2. The *Liaoning* is not merely intended for training and will be an operational platform of note in the PLA Navy's order of battle. It will also form the cornerstone around which China will build a major naval capability based on aircraft carriers.

3. The *Liaoning* is a poorly conceived naval project that will fail to meet its training, research or operational goals.

---

[15] Richards J. Heuer, "Strategic Deception and Counter-Deception: A Cognitive Process Approach," *International Studies Quarterly* 25, no.2, June 1981, 295, last accessed 3 June 2013, http://www.jstor.org/stable/2600359.

A conclusion on the most probable hypothesis will be arrived through the application of Heuer's theory which involves the falsification of hypotheses based on the availability of contrary evidence.

I.   CONCLUSION

The thesis concludes with an exploration of the implications of the findings of this study and recommendations for the tracking of future capability developments by China. Through the analyses provided in the thesis, the authors hope to improve understanding about China's strategic psyche, its employment of strategic deception and the intricacies of China's deception regarding the *Liaoning*. Through the deciphering of the *Liaoning* deception, enlightened policies can be formulated for dealing with the rising Chinese dragon in the East.

III. CHINA'S STRATEGIC PSYCHE AND NATIONAL SECURITY GOALS

A. INTRODUCTION

To understand the motivation behind the *Liaoning* Deception, it is necessary to understand China's perceived need for a major naval capability like the aircraft carrier. Naval capability is driven by China's strategic maritime goals which are determined by China's national security goals, which in turn are driven by national strategic goals. This chapter thus sets out to explain China's national security goals and explain their relation to her strategic maritime goals. It begins with a foray into five millennia of Chinese history and tradition to appreciate the strategic psyche of China and identify several traits that influence Chinese conception of strategy. This is followed by an examination of the national security goals of present-day China and how they relate to its maritime strategy.

Before proceeding, the qualification must be made that this chapter attempts to cover a lot of ground in very few pages. Much more comprehensive articles and books have been written on any given section of this chapter, so this chapter barely scratches the surface of its topics. Despite the lack of depth, this chapter attempts to identify critical and relevant features of the topics discussed for the uninitiated reader to make sense of the logic and causation of our hypothesis about Chinese strategic deception that will be discussed in subsequent chapters. This chapter does not summarize the extant arguments and perspectives for the topics highlighted. Interested readers are highly encouraged to dive deeper into the plethora of knowledge that is available out there.

Chronology of Chinese Civilization		
Dynasty	Period	Duration
Huang-di 黄帝	2690 - 2590 B.C.	100 years
Tang, Yao 唐尧	2333 - 2234 B.C.	100 years
Shun, Yu 虞舜	2233 - 2184 B.C.	50 years
Xia 夏	2183 - 1752 B.C.	432 years
Shang 商	1751 - 1111 B.C.	640 years
Zhou 周 -- Western Zhou 西周 1111 - 771 B.C. Eastern Zhou 东周 770 - 256 B.C. Spring and Autumn Period 春秋 700 - 40 B.C. Warring States Period 战国 403 - 221 B.C.		341 years 515 years
Qin 秦	221 - 206 B.C.	15 years
Han 汉 -- Western Han 西汉 206 B.C. - 8 A.D. New Han 新汉 9 - 23 Eastern Han 东汉 25 - 220		214 years 15 years 196 years
Three Kingdoms 三国 220-280 Wei 魏 220-265, Shu 蜀 221-263 , Wu 吴 222-280		60 years
Jin 晋 -- Western Jin 西晋 265-316 Eastern Jin 东晋 317-420		52 years 104 years
Northern and Southern Dynasties 南北朝 -- Southern Dynasties 南朝 Song 宋 420-479, Qi 齐 479-502 Liang 梁 502-557, Chen 陈 557-589 -- Northern Dynasties 北朝 Northern Wei 北魏 386-534, Eastern Wei 东魏 534-550 Western Wei 西魏 535-557, Northern Qi 北齐 550-557 Northern Chou 北周 557-581		
Sui 隋	581-618	38 years
Tang 唐	618-907	290 years
Five Dynasties and Ten Countries 五代十国 -- Five Dynasties 五代 Later Liang 后梁 907-923, Later Tang 后唐 923-936, Later Chin 后晋 936-946, Later Han 后汉 947-950, Later Chou 后周 951-960 -- Ten Countries 十国 902-979		
Song 宋 -- Northern Song 北宋 960-1127 Southern Song 南宋 1127-1279 Liao 辽 916-1125		167 years 153 years 210 years
西夏 Western Xia	1038-1227	190 years
金 Jin	1115-1234	120 years
元 Yuan	1279-1368	90 years
明 Ming	1368-1644	277 years
清 Qing	1644-1911	268 years
The Republic of China 中华民国 (Taiwan)	1912-Now	
The People's Republic of China 中华人民共和国	1949-Now	

Table 1.   Chronology of Chinese Civilization

B.   STRATEGIC PSYCHE OF THE CHINESE NATION

Modern China claims unbroken lineage to five millennia of tumultuous but continuous civilizational history (Table 1), seeking in its heritage not only deep nationalistic and civilizational pride but also reference to classical principles of strategy and statesmanship that continue to shape the thoughts and actions of modern Chinese leaders.[16]   Although many nations also justifiably claim long and eventful histories, few have preserved their written, oral and cognitive traditions as the Chinese civilization has, and fewer still actively use this heritage as a fundamental fountain of knowledge, experience and wisdom for society and its leaders.[17]   In fact, respected statesman Kissinger assesses that China is singular because:

> In no other country is it conceivable that a modern leader would initiate a major national undertaking by invoking strategic principles from a millennium-old event—nor that he would confidently expect his colleagues to understand the significance of his allusions.[18]

Understanding this state of Chinese civilizational self-awareness is paramount to making the first step towards an understanding of the Chinese strategic psyche. Chinese strategy involves the utilization of "history as a mirror to guide the present"—not just recent contemporary history but civilizational history going back millennia.[19]   Although it may seem that ancient history is irrelevant to the strategic considerations of a modern nation-state, in the case of China, there is good reason to appreciate the importance of Chinese civilizational memory and culture in shaping modern Chinese strategic psyche. This appreciation is important because unless one can put himself into the shoes of his adversary, attempts to understand the adversary would be futile. By understanding that the Chinese strategic psyche is not only driven by modernity but also antiquity opens up

---

[16] Classical Chinese texts, strategists, intellectuals and leaders like the Daode Jing (道德经), Sun Tzu's Art of War , Confucious (Kongzi孔子), the Qin emperor Qin Shi Huang (秦始皇), even the Mongol conqueror Genghis Khan are an important part of Chinese consciousness and often quoted and used as references for intellectual discussions, policy formulation and decision-making.

[17] C.P. Fitzgerald, *The Chinese View of Their Place in the World* (London: Oxford University Press, 1966): 2.

[18] Kissinger, *On China*, 2.

[19] Shi Naian, *The Water Margin: Outlaws of the Marsh* (Hong Kong: Tuttle Publishing, 2010), xxxvi.

an entire realm of possibilities that may explain Chinese strategic motives where contemporary explanations have faltered.

The second aspect of Chinese strategic psyche that requires understanding is also concerned with the temporal—but concerns not of looking backward in time as the first, but *forward* in time not just in years, but decades, even generations. The two temporally divergent perspectives (looking back and casting forward) are intimately related and it can be argued that the first influences the second. Due to the fact that the Chinese have an extended retrospective view of their civilization, they also adopt a long term perspective when considering the future. Chinese cognizance of the ebbs and flows of their own history tempers their hunger for rapidly-achieved but short-lived success.[20] Instead, the Chinese are wont to scheme protracted "multi-year maneuvers" that may not consist of singular decisive battlefield victories but rather an eclectic orchestra of political, military, economic and diplomatic actions that are designed to shape the whole strategic environment and render the adversary's military prowess ineffective.[21]

The third aspect of Chinese strategic psyche is a product of the strategic patience that undergirds their extended temporal perspective—the employment of the indirect approach. Kissinger observed that the Chinese *"stressed subtlety, indirection, and the patient accumulation of relative advantage."*[22] He illustrated this Chinese quality by contrasting the intellectual games of strategy favored by Chinese and Western civilizations—Weiqi[23] (围棋) and chess respectively. The Western game of chess is designed around the direct strategic approach. Game play commences with the set-piece array of forces on either side and evolves towards decisive engagements targeted at the opponent's center of gravity and elimination of key pieces, with victory achieved by capture of the opponent's king. In Weiqi, all pieces are of equal value and immobile - and

---

[20] Guanzhong Luo. *Three Kingdom,* abridged ed., trans. Moss Roberts (New Jersey: University of California Press, 2004), 1. One of the four Chinese classics, *The Romance of the Three Kingdoms* opens with: "The empire, long divided, must unite; long united, must divide."

[21] Kissinger, *On China*, 23.

[22] Kissinger, *On China*, 23.

[23] The Chinese translation of Weiqi literally means "Envelopment Chess", in reference to the gameplay where both sides stake territory on the board and attack the other side through envelopment of the opponent's pieces.

forces do not begin arrayed for decisive battle. The game begins with the board empty and game play involves the placement of immobile pieces on the board. Victory is dependent upon the domination of space on the board through strategic encirclement. Multiple engagements can take place anywhere within the battle-space and the significance of battle outcomes is often difficult to assess, with each side making gains of relative advantage rather than absolute ones. Victory is achieved through indirect means and strategic ambiguity and flexibility about the center of gravity of one's efforts is critical to success.[24]

The telling contrast between these strategic games provides a glimpse into Chinese strategic appreciation of the indirect approach. Sun Tzu alluded to the indirect strategy in his treatise when he said: "Those adept in warfare can conquer the enemy without fighting battles, capture cities without laying siege to them, and annex states without prolonged warfare. They can preserve their own forces whole and intact while struggling for the mastery of the entire Empire. They can win a victory without wearying their men. All this is due to strategy."[25]

Liddell Hart, the West's proponent of indirect warfare said of the indirect approach to warfare:

---

[24] Kissinger, *On China*, 25.

[25] Ta-Wei Yu, *Sun Tzu on the Art of War* (Taiwan: Li Ming, 1991), 68.

"In strategy, the longest way round is often the shortest way there; a direct approach to the object exhausts the attacker and hardens the resistance by compression, whereas an indirect approach loosens the defender's hold by upsetting his balance."[26]

Both Sun Tzu's and Hart's justifications for the wisdom of the indirect approach makes sense for China as it attempts to enhance its strategic position in an Asia-Pacific environment that is dominated by the U.S. (in Japan and South Korea) and in the face of obstacles that could conceivably be erected by its strategic competitors in the region and beyond. China's employment of the indirect approach to strategy would not only make its strategic goals more achievable, it would also mask them from detection and disruption by virtue of their indirect lines. The employment of strategic deception by the Chinese is also a manifestation of the indirect approach.

Last, Sun Tzu advised that "to win a war by defeating the enemy on the battlefield is not the most desirable. To vanquish the enemy without resort to warfare is the ultimate victory."[27] This proposes that strategic defeat of one's adversary is of greater value than simple military defeat on the battlefield. Therefore, in the Chinese formulation of strategy, military victory is never the most important, nor most salient consideration. Other influential factors such as diplomacy, economics, geography and society are considered and coordinated to secure lasting strategic victory. This does not mean that military action is unimportant in Chinese strategic thought, it emphasizes that the Chinese would consider military action in concert with other means to achieve their strategic goals.[28]

In summary, the Chinese strategic psyche possesses four relevant characteristics and their influence will be referred to throughout this thesis.

1.   History serves as a mirror to guide present strategy formulation.

---

[26] B.H. Liddell Hart, *Thoughts on War* (London: Faber and Faber, 1944), 239.

[27] Translation is authors' own after examination of other translations and in consideration of applicability to the discussion on China's strategic psyche. Original Chinese text is below.

"是故百战百胜，非善之善者也；不战而屈人之兵，善之善者也。"

[28] Andrew Scobell, "Strategic Culture and China: IR Theory versus the Fortune Cookie?" *Strategic Insights*, v.6, issue 10 (November 2005): 6, last accessed 3 June 2013, http://hdl.handle.net/10945/11404.

2.   Strategic patience and a very long term perspective inform planning and execution.

3.   The indirect approach to strategy and warfare is prevalent.

4.   Multi-faceted strategic victory is valued more than battlefield military victory.

C.   CHINA'S NATIONAL STRATEGIC GOALS

As the largest and arguably most successful communist nation today, it is far too easy to paint opinions about the Chinese nation in its infamous communist red—the primary color pre-dates its nationalistic communist associations and still symbolizes prosperity, blessings and positive energy for the Chinese people. Modern China has come to embrace both sides of its crimson identity—a fervent nationalism as well as a booming economy. This heady mix can fuel the aggressive nationalist ambitions as easily as it can improve the lives of 18% of the world population (China's 1.3 billion out of the world's 6.9 billion). [29] Where does the civilization that for millennia had considered itself to be superior in all important aspects (culture, education, sciences, governance, warfare) see its own destiny in the context of the current geo-strategic environment?[30] That is the question of this section.

In March 2013, Xi Jinping was confirmed as the President of the People's Republic of China and de-facto leader of the world's most populous nation. Xi's frequent references to the "China Dream" or Zhongguo Meng (中国梦) provide insight into what he perceives to be the national strategic goals of China.[31] The "China Dream" can be interpreted literally or figuratively. From a cultural and civilizational perspective, the China Dream can be interpreted as a revitalization or rejuvenation of the Chinese nation, the dawning of a new era of prosperity, happiness and strength.[32] The literal interpretation of the China Dream sets it up as a direct response to the contemporary

---

[29] Central Intelligence Agency, "The World Factbook: China," updated 7 May 2013, https://www.cia.gov/library/publications/the-world-factbook/geos/ch.html.

[30] Fitzgerald, *The Chinese View of Their Place in the World*, 7.

[31] Russell Leigh Moses, "Now Sharper, Xi Jinping's 'China Dream' Marks Departure From Past," *Wall Street Journal*, 3 April 2013, http://blogs.wsj.com/chinarealtime/2013/04/03/now-sharper-xi-jinpings-china-dream-marks-departure-from-past/.

[32] Moses, "Now Sharper, Xi Jinping's 'China Dream' Marks Departure From Past."

challenges faced by China—social tension and unrest due to inequitable wealth distribution, negative effects of unfettered economic development, and regional and global security challenges.[33] Thus, the China Dream literally desires to achieve the following national goals for China.

First, the China Dream aims to create a more equitable society—with more equitable wealth distribution in society and economic development within China. This is essential for the political survival of the Chinese Communist party because of the widespread and deep social unrest that can arise from a disaffected populace if the majority of the populace does not benefit from the economic gains.[34]

Second, sustainable and environmentally responsible development improves quality of living in China. Environmental damage, pollution and regional income disparities are obvious by-products of China's rapid economic development and have become major national concerns. Addressing sustainable development furthers China's credentials as a responsible country.

Third, China's development into a major military power is not merely driven by the pursuit of national status as a major power. It is also driven by the need to defend her sovereignty in regional territorial disputes and to protect her sprawling commercial interests that are increasingly spread around the globe.[35] Thus, national pride and economic interests are both of importance in guiding the development of China's military.

Having assessed the China Dream and its national strategic goals, we are in a better position to assess China's national security goals. One source for China's security policy is official pronouncements about China's policy and principles for dealing with other nations and her declared security interests. China has periodically released policy

---

[33] Moses, "Now Sharper, Xi Jinping's 'China Dream' Marks Departure From Past."

[34] David Pilling, "Xi Must Show He Can Deliver the 'China Dream'," *Financial Times*, 25 Apr 2013: 7.

[35] Jeremy Page, "For Xi, a 'China Dream' of Military Power," *Wall Street Journal*, Eastern edition, 13 March 2013: A.1.

statements pertaining to issues of regional and global interest that serve as a rich source of insight into China's national security objectives.

In September 2011, China published the White Paper "China's Peaceful Development" in which "China declared solemnly again to the world that peaceful development is a strategic choice made by China to realize modernization, make itself strong and prosperous, and make more contribution to the progress of human civilization."[36] China's commitment to peace serves national goals as well as more altruistic desires for world peace and civilizational progress—with national goals being the primary objective, and humankind's betterment a convenient by-product. A peaceful environment allows for China to devote resources to national economic growth and support not just a prosperous populace but the construction of a powerful military that will give the Chinese nation strength.

Tracking the rise of China in the post Deng era, the Chinese have largely been truthful in their statement—building a strong and prosperous nation have indeed been their goals and the strategy of peaceful development their method. However, to assume that China is inherently pacifist would be naive. Although Chinese assertiveness has largely been confined to regional territorial disputes, China has demonstrated resolve and a willingness to up the military ante in order to achieve her policy objectives— particularly with Taiwan, Japan and Vietnam.[37] This suggests that the preservation of territorial integrity and assertion of territorial rights is an important national strategic goal.

On 16 April 2013, China released its eighth Defense White Paper and the first policy paper since new Chinese President Xi Jinping took over the reins from Hu Jintao

---

[36] *China's Peaceful Development*, Information Office of the State Council.

[37] Taiwan: From 2000 to 2008, cross-straits relations were tense due to the election of a pro-independence Taiwanese President. China passed the Anti-Secession Law in 2005 which formalized non-peaceful means as a policy option in response to a declaration of independence by Taiwan.

Japan: On-going naval confrontations at sea over the disputed Senkaku Islands or Diao'yu Tai (钓鱼台) between China and Japan have caused relations between the traditional rivals to extremely tense.

Vietnam: In June 2012, Vietnam passed laws placing the Spratly and Paracel Islands under Vietnamese jurisdiction. At the same time, China passed laws establishing the prefecture of Sansha City which encompasses the Spratly, Paracel and Zhongsha islands. Both countries have called the other's moves illegal and invalid; keeping tensions between the two traditional antagonists still high.

in March 2013. The first section of the paper outlined the "new situation" and "new challenges" that confront China today and serve as the backdrop for "new missions" for China's armed forces. In reference to the "new situation" faced by China, the paper highlighted "signs of increasing hegemonism, power politics and neo-interventionism" in the world.[38] It also noted that the Asia-Pacific region had become a significant area for global economic development as well as "strategic interaction between major powers."[39] It is important to note that the aforementioned situations identified in the Defense White Paper were seen as exceptions to the broader landscape of peace and development as the "underlying trends of our time" and that "international forces are shifting in favor of maintaining world peace."[40] This is important as it demonstrates that China is self-aware about its own role in perpetuating the necessary conditions for development and progress of not just China, but the region and the world.

The "new challenge" for China is safeguarding its "national unification, territorial integrity and developmental interests."[41] Those three terms are coded references to Taiwan, territorial disputes with regional countries and China's burgeoning global economic interests. Three threats specifically identified in the White Paper were separatism, extremism and terrorism. These threats can be matched with each of the three challenges respectively—separatist sentiments in Taiwan, extreme nationalism in Japan and India, extreme religious beliefs in Tibet and Xinjiang that undermine territorial integrity and threaten economic interests.

What is really "new" in the strategic situation for China? Many of the threats that challenge China today are not "new" because the Taiwan issue, regional territorial disputes and unrest in its restive provinces have been extant issues for China. We believe the "new" paradigm stems from three major factors. First, the U.S. re-balancing of its military forces to the Pacific has increased U.S. presence and increased China's sense of

---

[38] *The Diversified Employment of China's Armed Forces*, Information Office of the State Council of the People's Republic of China, 16 April 2013, http://www.china.org.cn/government/whitepaper/node_7181425.htm.

[39] *The Diversified Employment of China's Armed Forces*, Information Office of the State Council.

[40] *The Diversified Employment of China's Armed Forces*, Information Office of the State Council.

[41] *The Diversified Employment of China's Armed Forces*, Information Office of the State Council.

insecurity. Second, improved Chinese military and national capabilities and their global reach have caused a corresponding expansion of the Chinese strategic outlook regionally and internationally.[42] Third, the Chinese economy is now a major component of the Asia Pacific economy and an important driver for the recovery of the developed world's lackluster economies. China's international stature has been rising throughout the new millennium, and watershed events like the 2008 Beijing Olympics and the growth of China's economy to be second only to the U.S. have served only to underline China's ascension to the world stage as a political, economic and military power. When the collective outcome of these developments is contrasted with the "old" Chinese paradigm that was a lot more insular and less assertive internationally, we begin to understand why the Chinese perceive this era as a "new" and exciting one.

The "new" paradigm that pervades Chinese strategic self-perception derives much from recent positive strategic developments for China coupled with increased emphasis on the Asia-Pacific region by the United States. This Chinese self-perception while not inherently dangerous has the potential to fuel Chinese military development and political assertiveness as a rising China flexes its political and economic muscle in East Asia, backed by an increasingly capable military force. Despite Chinese assurances that it does not seek hegemony, its assertiveness on issues like territorial disputes and U.S. presence in the region can be expected to grow stronger with time as China grows more confident. Zheng Wang explained the roles that the psychology of the Chinese civilization and its institutional memory play in China's self-perception of its 'China Dream'—which is constructed within the narrative of civilizational rejuvenation (fuxing复兴) rather than just being a mere national dream of a new generation of political elite.[43]

With our understanding of China's strategic psyche, national consciousness and national strategic goals, we can analyze the national security goals of China. In its 2013 Defense White Paper, China identified five fundamental operational principles for its armed forces:[44]

---

[42] From 2000 to 2013, China developed its indigenous satellite navigation system, launched its first manned space flight, successfully tested an anti-satellite missile, deployed its Navy for counter-piracy operations in the Horn of Africa and most recently launched its first aircraft carrier.

[43] Zheng Wang, "Not Rising, but Rejuvenating: The "Chinese Dream," *The Diplomat*, 5 February 2013, http://thediplomat.com/2013/02/05/chinese-dream-draft/.

[44] *The Diversified Employment of China's Armed Forces*,Information Office of the State Council.

1. Safeguarding national sovereignty, security and territorial integrity; and supporting the country's peaceful development.

2. Aiming to win local wars under conditions of informationization and expanding Chinese military preparedness.[45]

3. Provide comprehensive security and effective conduct of military operations other than war.

4. Deepening security cooperation and fulfilling international obligations.

5. Acting in accordance with laws, policies and military discipline.

Combining our understanding of the "China Dream," China's own assessment of her strategic challenges and position; and the operational principles for her armed forces; we assess China's national security goals as borne out in her Defense White Paper as the following (in descending order of priority):

1. Defending national sovereignty, security and territorial integrity

2. Supporting national economic and social development

3. Safeguarding world peace and global security[46]

D. RELATIONSHIP BETWEEN NATIONAL SECURITY GOALS AND THE MARITIME DOMAIN

In concert with her national security goals and the fundamental operational principles of her armed forces, China articulated the diverse roles expected of its armed forces. This section examines the link between the roles of China's armed forces and the maritime domain; and serves as a prelude to the next chapter on China's maritime strategy and how the aircraft carrier fits therein.

---

[45] Informationization refers to information-based warfare for China.

[46] Michael D. Swaine, "Does China Have a Grand Strategy?" *China: Contemporary Political, Economic, and International Affairs* (New York: NYU Press, 2007), 40. This goal appears too altruistic to be true and perhaps may be code for "attaining geopolitical influence as a primary state in the Asia-Pacific region and possibly beyond" – as postulated by Swaine in his work on China's grand strategy objectives.

Table 2.   Roles of China's Armed Forces

Roles of China's Armed Forces		
First Priority	**Second Priority**	**Third Priority**
Defending national sovereignty, security and territorial integrity	**Supporting national economic and social development**	**Safeguarding world peace and regional stability**
Sub-Tasks		
Safeguard border and coastal security	Participate in national development	Participate in UN peace keeping operations
Safeguard territorial air security	Participate in emergency rescue and disaster relief	International disaster relief and humanitarian aid
Maintaining constant combat readiness	Maintain social stability	Safeguarding the security of international SLOCs
Carry out scenario based exercises and drills	Safeguard maritime rights and interests	Joint exercise and training with foreign armed forces
	Protecting overseas interests	

Source: *The Diversified Employment of China's Armed Forces*, Information Office of the State Council of the People's Republic of China, 16 April 2013.

An analysis of the roles of China's Armed Forces shows that in each of the three priority categories, there are roles that require maritime capabilities because they either take place in the maritime domain or the seas provide the best or primary means of approach. The roles in blue font require sea control to be established and the ability for China to project maritime forces into the areas of concern. The roles in red font require maritime support (not necessarily amounting to sea control) because the maritime domain may be an important part of such operations (territorial air security and disaster relief) or because the maritime domain may constitute a major component of such efforts (naval exercises and training). These maritime-related roles have been organized into a separate table below. It is clear that the maritime capability of China's PLAN will need to be capable of large-scale blue water operations to fulfill some of the national security roles that have been identified.

Table 3.   Maritime Roles of China's Armed Forces

Roles where Sea Control is required	Roles where Maritime Support may be required
Safeguard border and coastal security	Safeguard territorial air security
Safeguard maritime rights and interests	Participate in emergency rescue and disaster relief
Protecting overseas interests	International disaster relief and humanitarian aid
Safeguarding the security of international SLOCs	Joint exercise and training with foreign armed forces

Examining the roles where sea control will be required, the correlation of these roles with control of the maritime domain is clear. For safeguarding border and coastal security, some measure of security can be established ashore. However, a shored-based strategy would be defensively static and unable to influence the maritime domain where threat vectors may ingress or egress. To effectively perform coastal security, China needs to be able to establish control over a defined maritime space for a defined temporal period, or at the very least deny that maritime space to its adversaries.[47] These roles are easier to support from ashore with a brown-water maritime force because the maritime space is only a means of access to shore-based interests. In order to safeguard maritime rights/interests overseas and the Sea Lines of Communications (SLOCs) that may be located far from the coast, China will require a longer range, higher endurance, more capable blue-water force that can operate far from the coast at extended periods.[48]

For the roles where maritime support may be required and sea control not necessarily achieved, the requirements for long range, high endurance are not as important as the ability of the maritime platforms to support the roles. Safeguarding territorial air security includes maritime airspace that requires ships with effective aerial surveillance radars and surface to air weapon systems. Whether supporting disaster and humanitarian relief operations domestically or abroad, the PLAN will need to be able to move large quantities of material at short notice and facilitate access to inaccessible areas. Joint exercises and training require the least overheads in terms of specialized capabilities—but navies in particular are especially valuable for such interactions due to their self-contained nature (minimal requirements for physical relocation of men and material) and the long tradition of naval cooperation and exercise at sea.

E.   CONCLUSION

This chapter has provided a glimpse into the various elements that influence China's strategic considerations. Important elements of Chinese strategic psyche were

---

[47] Bernard D. Cole, *The Great Wall at Sea*, (Annapolis, Maryland: Naval Institute Press, 2001), 159.

[48] *The Diversified Employment of China's Armed Forces*, Information Office of the State Council.

examined. China's national strategic goals were laid out by examining statements made by the latest generation of Chinese leaders on the "Chinese Dream," as well as China's policy for peaceful development. China's national security goals were identified based on the latest Defense White Paper and the roles of China's armed forces examined for their relation to the maritime domain. By studying the macro-level influences at the cultural, national and strategic levels that influence strategic goals, this chapter sets the stage for an in-depth analysis of China's maritime strategy and deception strategies in the next two chapters.

THIS PAGE INTENTIONALLY LEFT BLANK.

IV. CHINA'S MARITIME HERITAGE & STRATEGY

A. INTRODUCTION

This chapter examines China's contemporary maritime strategy and the role of aircraft carriers in that strategy. It begins with a brief study of China's maritime heritage to understand the historical evolution of what is currently known as the People's Liberation Army Navy (PLAN). Knowledge of China's maritime heritage contributes to the understanding of PLAN's development trajectory and the evolution of Chinese maritime strategic thought. The source and substance of current Chinese maritime strategy will be examined before the role of the aircraft carrier in complementing that strategy is explained. The objective of this chapter is to explain the utility of the aircraft carrier to China's maritime strategy and verify its credentials as a critical naval capability for China.

B. MARGINALIZATION OF CHINESE NAVAL DEVELOPMENT IN EARLY CHINESE HISTORY

The history of warfare throughout Chinese history has predominantly been a history of land warfare. For imperial China, the inland plains and valleys were where empires were made and emperors crowned. The vast seas served only as conduits for trade and exploration.[49] In post-imperial republican China, the seas became the medium through which dominance was exerted by Europe and Japan along China's coast through trade and naval power. Even then, the existence of Chinese civilization was never seriously threatened by China's maritime weakness. Finally, the Communists under Mao defeated the Kuomintang (KMT) through their campaigns in China's hinterland before taking the coast and forcing the KMT across the Taiwan Straits. This historic Chinese view of the utility (or lack thereof) of maritime power is shaped by Chinese strategic perspective on the centrality of their civilization and their geopolitical history. An understanding of these perspectives provides the foundation from which we can understand modern China's perspective on the utility of maritime power and command of the sea.

---

[49] None of the four major capitals of Chinese civilization (Chang'an, Loyang, Nanjing and Beijing) were located on the coast, all were inland cities.

For millennia, land warfare has been the dominant type of warfare that determined possession of the monopoly of power that emanated from the Chinese emperors. Maritime power and naval warfare only played minor roles in Chinese history. Even though imperial China possessed advance maritime science that surpassed that of any civilization between the tenth and fifteenth centuries, and sent vast imperial armadas halfway around the globe, imperial China's interest in the strategic value of the seas never materialized.[50] The seas offered little strategic value for imperial China. The main threats to the dynasties came overland from the Asian interior to the north and the west— all the crucial battles were fought on land.[51] When imperial navies did prosper (in the Song, Yuan and Ming dynasties), their missions were limited to coastal defense and control of maritime trade.[52] By the time the Qing dynasty felt seaborne pressure from European and Japanese fleets in the nineteenth century, the imperial navy had fallen far behind in contemporary naval capabilities and could do little to protect the Chinese coasts—contributing to the fall of the last imperial Chinese dynasty.

The post-imperial period of China was marked by a period when China was known as the "sick man of the East" (Dongya Bingfu东亚病夫) for its weakness and inability to defend itself against both Western powers and the Japanese—whose main access to China were through the Chinese coastal cities where the superior foreign navies reigned unchallenged. This painful memory of national subjugation and decline facilitated through domination by foreign navies would return to influence Chinese strategic considerations when China designed her maritime strategy.

Japan invaded China through Manchuria in 1937. Japanese maritime dominance in East Asia following her defeat of the Russian fleet at the 1905 Battle of Tsushima and Japanese subjugation of Port Arthur returned to haunt China. The eight years of resistance by both Chinese Nationalists and Communists was fought exclusively on land in China's interior as the Japanese Navy controlled China's coasts with impunity. Again,

---

[50] Cole, *The Great Wall at Sea*, 3. The fifteenth century Ming dynasty eunuch admiral Zheng He (郑和) took his vast fleet of ships as far as the Middle East and Africa – showcasing "Chinese shipbuilding, voyage management and navigation ability well beyond European capabilities."

[51] Cole, *The Great Wall at Sea*, 4.

[52] Cole, *The Great Wall at Sea*, 4.

in a battle for national survival, maritime strategy played no significant role except to serve as a painful reminder of China's weakness in the maritime arena.

After Japan's defeat in WWII, the Chinese civil war between the Nationalist KMT and Communists was fought in China's interior where Communist strongholds dominated and moved to the coast as KMT forces were pushed back. In 1949, when KMT forces withdrew to Taiwan, the Communists did not possess the maritime capabilities to pursue them decisively across the Taiwan Strait. Once more, China's maritime capability was outstanding for its irrelevance and ineptness.

The formative years of modern day China were therefore dominated by a succession of land wars that drove the Japanese invaders back and pushed the Nationalist KMT forces to Taiwan. The operational strategy, structure and capabilities of the PLA were therefore focused for warfare on land and not at sea. But the salience of the seas on China's national security would not be totally forgotten. The tumultuous period between the last Chinese imperial dynasty and communist triumph in China were sandwiched between two significant failures of maritime capability that allowed foreign navies free reign on China's coastline and the Nationalist KMT forces to escape to Taiwan.

C.   NAVAL DEVELOPMENT IN COMMUNIST CHINA

The fortunes of the PLAN improved from 1949 as the Chinese nation grew in stature domestically and internationally. In 1953, Mao Zedong raised the hopes of China's budding maritime force when he declared that "We must build a strong navy for the purpose of fighting against imperialist aggression."[53]

In 1949, the first PRC Navy was formed mainly from the defected Nationalist KMT Second Coastal Defense Fleet. Its role was to establish law and order on coastal and riverine waters, help capture offshore islands occupied by the KMT forces and prepare for the capture of Taiwan.[54] During the formative years of the PLAN, Soviet assistance in equipment acquisition, system design and doctrine formulation were

---

[53] Cole, *The Great Wall at Sea*, 10.

[54] Cole, *The Great Wall at Sea*, 17.

33

significant and would remain so until the Sino-Soviet split in 1960. Elimination of the KMT forces in Taiwan was still a major pre-occupation of Mao and drove the design and mission of the early PLAN.

The outbreak of the Korean War and the successful amphibious landings in Incheon by U.S. led United Nations forces in 1950 led to strategic reconsiderations about naval capabilities by China. However, Chinese strategic development was hampered by Mao's ideological insistence on the principle of "People's War" and the 1959 dismissal of Peng Dehuai who commanded Chinese forces in Korea and who was the chief proponent for China's strategic review.[55] Thus PLAN modernization and strategic refocus gave way to China's strategic focus on developing nuclear weapons and recovering from the disastrous "Great Leap Forward." An important development was the birth of the PLAN Air Force (PLANAF) in 1952 whose role was maritime air defense, anti-ship and anti-submarine operations. Nevertheless, the PLAN's strategic focus remained on maritime defense in coastal waters. In 1953, the PLAN Marine Corps was stood up with a single regiment's strength.[56] In 1955, Taiwan cited continuing threats from China to pressure the U.S. to enter into a mutual defense treaty, thereby creating a significant obstacle to future Chinese invasion of Taiwan. Not coincidentally, the division strength PLA Marine Corps was disbanded in 1957 despite the renaissance for amphibious forces elsewhere brought on by the successful Incheon landings in 1950.[57] The deconstruction of the PLA Marine Corps can be attributed to the U.S. - Taiwan mutual defense treaty, as well as the fact that by 1955, China had retaken the offshore islands that it could from the KMT: Hainan (海南), Wanshan (万山), Zhoushan(舟山), Yijiangshan (一江山) and Dachen (大陈).[58] Therefore, the raison d'etre for the PLAN Marine Corps was no longer valid—not until almost two decades later for islands farther down south in the South China Sea.

---

[55] Cole, *The Great Wall at Sea*, 20.

[56] Neng Tong, *Zhong'gong Haijun Xieshi* (中共海军写实) [(Beijing: Military Sciences Press, 1999), 250.

[57] Tong, *Zhong'gong Haijun Xieshi* (中共海军写实).

[58] Kissinger, *On China*, 156.

The Sino-Soviet split in 1960 threw back military modernization plans for the whole PLA force, hitting the hardware-oriented PLAN hard.[59] A short war with India in 1962 and military operations in Tibet continued to emphasize land-based warfare at the expense of the PLAN. Mao's ideology of "People's War" continued to hamper naval modernization as technology and hardware were seen as inferior to ideologically-driven soldiers.[60] Even the 1970 deployment of China's first Soviet-designed ballistic missile submarine (without nuclear missiles) did not increase modernization or resources available to the PLAN as nuclear weapons were a national military project and did not benefit the PLAN as a whole.[61] Most critically, this period of the Cultural Revolution (1966-76) retarded technological development in general and the PLAN would fall further behind in important developments in naval warfare that included the utilization of guided missiles for anti-surface, anti-air and anti-submarine warfare; computerization, command, control and intelligence (C3I) and automation in sensors and propulsion.[62] China would take decades to catch up in terms of both hardware upgrades and the professional education of its sailors.

The development of the PLAN under Mao was marked by general under-development and confinement to defensive maritime roles once Taiwan secured U.S. defense guarantees. The strategic role of the PLAN in China's national security strategy was marginal and only gained some importance with the 1970 deployment of China's first ballistic missile submarine. The PLAN was doctrinally backward and had missed major naval warfare developments. It was thus technologically behind its naval contemporaries and was in no shape to effectively project force into the Asian-Pacific region. Unfortunately for the PLAN, domestic political, social and economic turmoil derailed its development under Mao.

---

[59] Cole, *The Great Wall at Sea*, 22.

[60] Cole, *The Great Wall at Sea*, 23.

[61] Cole, *The Great Wall at Sea*, 23.

[62] Cole, *The Great Wall at Sea*, 23.

## D.	CHINA'S CONTEMPORARY NAVAL DEVELOPMENTS

Mao's death in 1976 and Deng Xiaoping's tenure marked the rehabilitation of China into the international system and the rebirth of the Chinese economy. China had plugged back into the world and was growing rapidly in many strategic areas. With internal stability and growing wealth, China looked to develop its air force and navy to create a modern and balanced military force. In 1979, Deng Xiaoping called for "a strong navy with modern combat capability."[63] Most significantly for the PLAN, Mao's doctrine of "People's War" was increasingly pushed back by recognition of the importance of technology and military hardware.

In the 1970s, Soviet naval prowess was at its height and Japanese naval capabilities were also improving. Fortunately and ironically, China was now re-engaging in bilateral relations with the U.S. by Nixon's 1972 visit.[64] In the context of the Cold War, the formidable U.S. Navy's Pacific Fleet was a more than adequate deterrent against the Soviet Pacific fleet. China also believed that the terms of the U.S. – Japan treaty would keep Japan's naval ambitions in check.[65] In 1974, the PLA's marginally successful naval action against South Vietnamese naval forces in the Paracels (Xisha 西沙[66]) proved to be of strategic importance but not because the small islets that were now under Chinese control. Rather, the incident strengthened Chinese strategic awareness about the importance of building credible force projection capabilities in the PLAN and awakened China's interest in protecting what it saw as its traditional sovereign territorial interests in the South China Sea. As a result, the PLAN's disbanded Marine Corps was reestablished in 1979 and assigned to the South Seas Fleet together with the PLAN's amphibious assets. In 1980 the South Seas Fleet conducted a major

---

[63] Cole, *The Great Wall at Sea*, 10.

[64] Kissinger, *On China*, 255.

[65] Cole, *The Great Wall at Sea*, 25.

[66] The Paracels are known by China as Xisha or "Western Sands". In addition, Macclesfield Bank is known by China as Zhongsha (中沙) or "Central Sands" and the Spratlys are known as Nansha (南沙) or "Southern Sands". Collectively, China terms the island groups as Sansha (三沙) or the "Three Sands".

fleet exercise focused on the seizure and defense of islands in the South China Sea—an exercise that has become a regular fixture in the PLAN training cycle.[67]

Cole credits three significant events in the 1980s that enhanced PLAN development. First was Deng Xiaoping's scathing review of the PLA's performance in the 1979 Sino-Vietnamese war. [68] Even though the PLAN was not directly involved in that war's operations, it benefited from the institutional review within the military to become more operationally effective. Second was the 1985 determination that the Soviet Union no longer posed a nuclear threat to China.[69] This resulted in the PLA's distancing from the continental strategy that marginalized the PLAN. The PLA was to prepare for "small wars on the periphery" instead and China's extensive maritime periphery improved the PLAN's ability to obtain resources within the PLA.[70] Third was the 1982 appointment of Liu Huaqing (刘华清) as PLAN commander. He promulgated a maritime strategy for the PLAN that allowed it to progress into modernity. He also led a widespread reorganization of the Navy, Marine Corps, research and development, and training systems.[71] During this period, the PLAN acquired extensive Western military technology and in 1988 successfully launched an intermediate range ballistic missile to confirm its ability to deploy strategic nuclear weapons at sea.[72] The collapse of the Soviet Union in 1989 removed a major land threat and provided further impetus for the PLA to improve maritime capabilities. It also opened up the possibility of acquiring former Soviet technology with greater ease.

In the 1990s, in addition to force modernization, the PLAN began long-range deployments to East and South Asia and sent a task group to visit the Western Hemisphere as well. The first Gulf War in 1990 demonstrated the superiority of U.S.

---

[67] Cole, *The Great Wall at Sea*, 25.

[68] Cole, *The Great Wall at Sea*, 26.

[69] Mikhail Gorbachev came to power in 1985 and oversaw a slew of reconciliation measures with China – including a reduction in USSR forces along the Sino-Soviet border, resumption of trade and cooling of border disputes.

[70] Cole, *The Great Wall at Sea*, 26.

[71] Cole, *The Great Wall at Sea*, 26.

[72] Chong-Pin Lin, "China's Military Modernization: Perceptions, Progress and Prospects," *Security Studies*, Volume 3, Issue 4, 1994, 726.

technology in overcoming conventional force advantages and prompted China to reevaluate its military development. The peaceful handover of Hong Kong to China in 1997 enhanced the importance of maritime security for China's economy and prompted Jiang Zemin to urge the PLAN to "build up the nation's maritime Great Wall."[73]

E. THE PLAN FORGES AHEAD IN THE NEW MILLENNIUM

The new millennium saw the PLAN fully emerge from its brown water Navy roots and deploy modern capabilities with an operational reach that extended beyond the Asia Pacific. It seemed that the PLAN had finally made up for its lost decades in the naval wilderness and had gained the confidence to operate alongside its modern naval contemporaries. Within its own maritime area of operations, the PLAN was also increasingly assertive and confident. Encouraging military modernization in 2006, Hu Jintao advised the the PLAN to "endeavor to build a powerful People's navy that can adapt to its historical mission during a new century and new period."[74]

The PLAN embraced regional and extra-regional operations with increasing frequency and significance—participating in a multitude of bilateral exercises with Asian and Western navies that enhanced its professionalism. In 2008, the PLAN deployed its first three-ship task group to the Gulf of Aden to participate in United Nations sanctioned counter-piracy operations. This marked the first time that Chinese naval ships were deployed for military operations outside the Asia-Pacific. China has since maintained a constant presence of PLAN ships in the Gulf of Aden to protect Chinese shipping interests.[75] In 2011, the frigate Xuzhou was dispatched from China's counter-piracy task

---

[73] Cole, *The Great Wall at Sea*, 11.

[74] Andrew S. Erickson and Michael S. Chase, "Informatization and the Chinese People's Liberation Army Navy," in *The Chinese Navy: Expanding Capabilities, Evolving Roles,* eds. Phillip C. Saunders, Christopher Yung, Michael Swaine, and Andrew Nien-dzu Yang (Washington, DC: Center for the Study of Chinese Military Affairs, Institute for National Strategic Studies, National Defense University, 2011), 247.

[75] Andrew S. Erickson and Austin M. Strange, "Learning the Ropes in Blue Water: The Chinese Navy's Gulf of Aden Deployments Have Borne Worthwhile Lessons in Far-Seas Operations—Lessons that Go Beyond the Antipiracy Mission," *Proceedings*, U.S. Naval Institute. (April 2013), 34-38.

group to successfully support non-combatant evacuation of Chinese nationals from Libya—thus demonstrating the operational agility and readiness of the PLAN.[76]

The PLAN also became the face of an increasingly assertive China in the Asia Pacific maritime arena. In areas where its sovereignty was perceived to be challenged, the PLAN had been unapologetic in asserting its freedom of action towards regional rivals Taiwan, Russia, Japan, Philippines and Vietnam. Sovereignty dispute incidents involving Chinese ships in the Asia Pacific started to increase. In 2007, China established 'Sansha City' (三沙市) on one of the disputed Paracel islands in the South China Sea to assert its sovereignty.[77]

Not only has China been increasingly assertive about maritime rights towards its regional neighbors, it has also challenged the U.S. hegemon in the Asia Pacific. Table 4 below shows the various incidents in maritime East Asia that have involved China. These incidents when assessed in toto reflect China's willingness to assert its sovereignty and challenge what it perceives to be U.S. freedom of action within China's area of influence.

---

[76] Gabe Collins, Andrew S. Erikson, "Implications of China's Military Evacuation of Citizens from Libya," *James Town Foundation: China Brief*, Volume 11 (4), 10 March 2011, http://www.jamestown.org/programs/chinabrief/single/?tx_ttnews%5Btt_news%5D=37633&cHash=7278c fd21e6fb19afe8a823c5cf88f07.

[77] Office of the Secretary of Defense, *Annual Report to Congress: Military Power of the People's Republic of China 2008,* last accessed 4 June 2013, http://www.defense.gov/pubs/pdfs/China_Military_Report_08.pdf.

Table 4.   Maritime Incidents Involving China

2001	April. Hainan Island incident: Mid-air collision between Chinese interceptor and U.S. surveillance plane.[1]
2006	China's State Oceanographic Administration's Marine Surveillance force begins regular patrols in the South China Sea. [2] China issues demarches to oil companies about exploration in South China Sea.[3]
2007	November. U.S. Navy ships' port call requests into Hong Kong rejected by China.[4]
2009	March. USNS Impeccable harassed by Chinese ships and aircraft in South China Sea.[5] May. USNS Victorious harassed by Chinese ships and aircraft in Yellow Sea.[6] China submits map with "nine-dashed line" to the United Nations Commissions on Limits of Continental Shelf.[7] June. Chinese submarine collides with USN destroyer's towed array sonar off Subic Bay.[8]
2010	August. First Chinese midget submarine plants flag on bottom of South China Sea.[9] November. PLAN South Sea Fleet conducts amphibious assault exercise in South China Sea.
2011	May. Chinese ships cut cable of Vietnamese oil exploration ship in South China Sea.[10]
2012	March. Second Chinese midget submarine plants second flag on bottom of South China Sea.[11] July. China establishes Sansha City and sets up military garrison on Yongxing Island in the Paracels.[12] December. Chinese province issues rules allowing interception of ships in South China Sea.[13]
2013	January. PLAN ship locks fire-control radar on Japanese ship off Senkaku Islands.[14]

Sources:

[1] Shirley A. Kan *et al.*, *China-U.S. Aircraft Collision Incident of April 2001: Policy Implications*, CRS Report RL30946 (Washington , D.C: Library of Congress, Congressional Research Service, 10 October 2001).

[2] Michael D. Swaine, *China's Maritime Disputes in the East and South China Seas*, 4 April 2013, U.S.-China Economic and Security Review Commission, last accessed 4 June 2013, http://carnegieendowment.org/2013/04/04/maritime-disputes-must-be-carefully-managed/fxea#.

[3] Swaine, *China's Maritime Disputes in the East and South China Seas*, 4 April 2013, U.S.-China Economic and Security Review Commission, http://carnegieendowment.org/2013/04/04/maritime-disputes-must-be-carefully-managed/fxea#.

[4] "China tells more U.S. vessels to keep out," *Central News Network*, 30 November 2007, http://edition.cnn.com/2007/US/11/30/china.us/.

[5] Raul Pedrozo, "Close Encounters at Sea: The USNS Impeccable Incident," *Naval War College Review*, Summer 2009, Vol.62, No.3.

Continued on next page.

Continued from previous page.

[6] Barbara Starr, "Chinese Boats harassed U.S. ship, officials say," *Central News Network*, 5 May 2009, http://edition.cnn.com/2009/WORLD/asiapcf/05/05/china.maritime.harassment/index.html.

[7] Beckman and Tara Davenport, "CLCLS submissions and claims to the South China Sea," *South China Sea Studies,* last modified 16 August 2011, http://southchinaseastudies.org/en/conferences-and-seminars-/second-international-workshop/608-clcs-submissions-and-claims-in-the-south-china-sea-by-robert-c-beckman-a-tara-davenport.

[8] Barbara Starr, "Sub collides with sonar array towed by U.S. navy ship," *Central News Network*, 12 June 2009, http://www.cnn.com/2009/US/06/12/china.submarine/.

[9] "China plants flag beneath South China Sea," *United Press International,* 26 August 2010, http://www.upi.com/Top_News/US/2010/08/26/China-plants-flag-beneath-South-China-Sea/UPI-27691282870074/.

[10] Jane Perlez, "Dispute flares over energy in South China Sea," *The New York Times*, 4 December 2012, http://www.nytimes.com/2012/12/05/world/asia/china-vietnam-and-india-fight-over-energy-exploration-in-south-china-sea.html?_r=0.

[11] Stephen Chen, "Submarine plants flag on ocean floor," *South China Morning Post*, 30 March 2012, http://www.scmp.com/article/723202/submarine-plants-flag-ocean-floor.

[12] Austin Ramzy, "China's newest city raises threat of conflict in South China Sea," *Time*, 24 July 2012, http://world.time.com/2012/07/24/chinas-newest-city-raises-threat-of-conflict-in-the-south-china-sea/.

[13] Jane Perlez, "Alarm as China issues rules for disputed area," *New York Times*, 1 December 2012, http://www.nytimes.com/2012/12/02/world/asia/alarm-as-china-issues-rules-for-disputed-sea.html?_r=0.

[14] "China military officials admit radar lock on Japanese ship," *South China Morning Post,* 18 March 2013, http://www.scmp.com/news/china/article/1193600/china-military-officials-admit-radar-lock-japanese-ship?page=all.

China's military technology made substantive strides in the first decade of the new millennium —deploying capabilities that have the potential for strategic effects. The Beidou global positioning navigation system became operational in 2000. China's anti-satellite missile was successfully demonstrated in 2007 to serve warning. China deployed its first anti-carrier ballistic missile as a deterrent to U.S. carriers in 2009. [78] In 2012, China commissioned its first aircraft carrier. Thus, the rash of technological and capability advancements by China in the first decade of the new millennium were nothing short of extraordinary.

The significance of the PLAN to China's national security has been enhanced in the new millennium by its expanded roles, capabilities and operational effects.

---

[78] "Chinese develop special 'Kill Weapon' to destroy U.S. aircraft carriers," *U.S. Naval Institute*, 31 March 2009, http://www.usni.org/news-and-features/chinese-kill-weapon.

In April 2013, Xi Jinping advised the PLAN to "enhance its preparedness for combat" when he made a highly symbolic visit to the PLAN's Southern Fleet shortly after he took office in March 2013.[79]

What accounts for the unprecedented growth in the PLAN's capabilities after the 1980s and what maritime strategy drove its deployment?

F.   CHINA'S MARITIME STRATEGY

Liu Huaqing who served as PLAN commander from 1982 to 1988 has been identified as the father of the modern PLAN due to his influence on its modernization, development and strategic deployment. 'China's Mahan' has been recognized as the intellectual engine behind China's maritime strategy that provided the foundation for the PLAN's modernization, expansion and relevance to China's national security.[80]

In 1985, Liu launched China's maritime strategy and explained that the top objectives were to protect territorial sovereignty, legal maritime rights and natural resources in the Yellow Sea, East China Sea, and South China Sea.[81] The critical pillars of Liu's maritime strategy that are relevant to this thesis are:

- **Offshore Defense** (近海防御). Defining offshore operations as occurring within the first island chain, Liu extended beyond the near-coast defense (近岸防御) limitation common in China's naval heritage, yet limited unwise over reach that would challenge the global ocean-faring capabilities of the Soviet or U.S. navies.[82]

- **Strategic Defense.** A strategic maritime defense line will be maintained through offensive naval operations to engage threats far from the Chinese coast. This strategic defense line can stretch to the second island chain if the PLAN's capabilities are up to the task.

---

[79] Yang Fang, "President Xi calls for strengthened navy," *Xinhua* (China), 11 April 2013, http://news.xinhuanet.com/english/china/2013-04/11/c_132301838.htm.

[80] James R. Holmes and Toshi Yoshihara, *Chinese Naval Strategy in the 21st Century: The turn to Mahan* (New York: Routledge, 2008), 41.

[81] Holmes, *Chinese Naval Strategy in the 21st Century: The turn to Mahan*, 31.

[82] The first island chain extends from the Kurile islands through Japan's main islands, the Ryuku Archipelago, Taiwan, Philippines to Borneo.

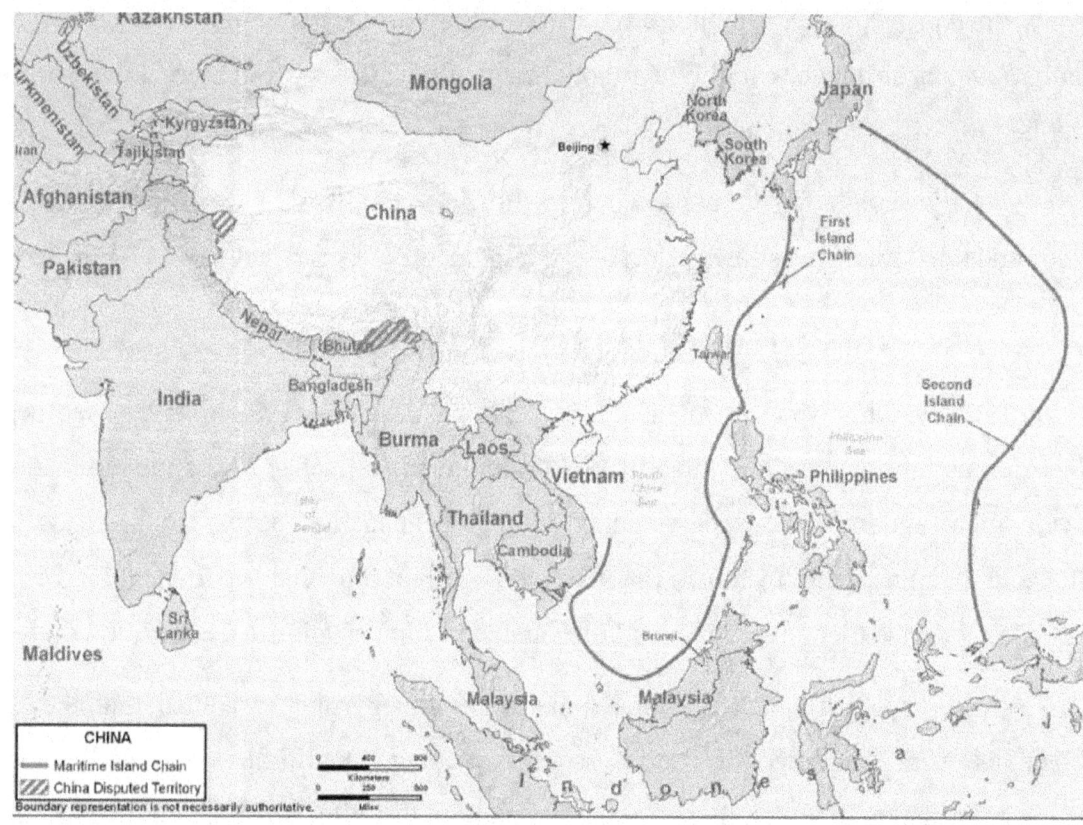

Figure 1: China's Strategic Island Chains[83]

Liu's strategic foresight was not the only factor that led to the adoption of this ambitious maritime strategy for the PLAN. The strategic environment in the mid-1980s that supported this maritime strategy also played an important role.[84] External factors included fundamental changes in China's external security environment—like the diminished strategic threat posed by the Soviet Union, the rising capabilities of regional navies and increasing national interest in maritime resources. Internal factors included the "loosening of doctrinaire views in the post-Mao era, Deng Xiaoping's investment of political capital in modernizing the Chinese military," and China's rapidly growing economic wealth.[85]

---

[83] Office of the Secretary of Defense, *Military Power of the People's Republic of China 2008*, 25.

[84] OSD, *Military Power of the People's Republic of China 2008*, 32.

[85] OSD, *Military Power of the People's Republic of China 2008*, 26.

It is no coincidence that Liu's maritime strategy fits with the latest outline of the roles envisaged for the PLAN and China's current national security goals that were outlined in Chapter II.[86] The post 1980 evolution of the PLAN was planned with Liu's maritime strategy as a guide. Thus, the PLAN's capabilities today are a result of calculated strategic planning and execution, resulting in the PLAN's fulfillment of the strategic functions for which it was designed.

China's maritime strategy also deals with a legion of potential threats to its "national unification, territorial integrity and development interests."[87] "National unification" refers to China's espoused desire to re-unite with Taiwan, China has termed pro-independence Taiwanese elements as separatist forces. "Territorial integrity" refers to disputes with Japan over the Senkaku Islands; with the Indians over Arunachal Pradesh and Aksai Chin; and with some Southeast Asian states over the Spratly and Paracel islands in the South China Sea. It is noteworthy that of the three major territorial disputes engulfing China today, two are maritime in nature—Senkaku and the South China Sea. "Development interests" include maritime resources located in disputed areas in the East China Sea and South China Sea; and the Sea Lines of Communications (SLOC) that ensure the safe movement of goods and resources critical to China's globalized economy.

Given the trajectory of the PLAN's development in the new millennium, the salience of Liu Huaqing's outward looking maritime strategy, and China's maritime strategic interests, the inclusion of aircraft carriers into the PLAN's order of battle should have come as no surprise to observers.

G. SALIENCE OF AIRCRAFT CARRIERS TO CHINA'S MARITIME STRATEGY

Navies are built around ships of various sizes and ability—the tension between size and vulnerability remaining unchanged even as naval warfare has advanced. Despite the reach of orbiting satellites and long-range missiles, the enduring power of presence on the high seas remains synonymous with command and control of the maritime domain.

---

[86] *The Diversified Employment of China's Armed Forces*, Information Office of the State Council.

[87] *The Diversified Employment of China's Armed Forces*, Information Office of the State Council.

44

Modern naval warfare takes place in the air, on the surface and under the waves. The carrier and submarine campaigns of the Second World War, Falklands War and Cold War continue to remind us that no matter how high-tech militaries may become, the ability to fight effectively in all three mediums is essential to strategic success. In China's case, the PLAN has developed into a modern navy with ships and submarines of varying size and capability. The most glaring omission in the PLAN order of battle until 2012 was the absence of an aircraft carrier.

Understanding the PLAN's difficult transition from a backward coastal force to a sea-going naval fleet towards the end of the 20th century, it is hardly surprising that an aircraft carrier capability was not developed earlier. The aircraft carrier is an extremely resource-intensive capability—not only is the ship itself an engineering monstrosity, operations onboard the aircraft carrier require a level of professionalism and skill within the Navy that cannot be built overnight and require mastery of other aspects of naval operations that will support an aircraft carrier. Aircraft carriers do not operate in isolation because they are such vulnerable high value targets that they require additional ships normally found in a carrier battle group to secure an air, surface and sub-surface protective bubble around the carrier. The PLAN therefore had to reach a substantive level of maturity before it could realistically conceive of operating an aircraft carrier. Not only did the PLAN need sufficient numbers of vessels to form a carrier battle group, they needed to be sufficiently capable in multi-dimensional naval warfare to be effective. The PLAN's meteoric development after the 1980s is assessed to have brought it to the force size and capability levels sufficient to operate an aircraft carrier.[88] Taking the next developmental step of building an aircraft carrier capability was therefore a logical next step for the PLAN.

Conceptually, the aircraft carrier is not alien to Chinese maritime strategy. Liu Huaqing advocated the strengths of an aircraft carrier capability to strengthen the PLAN's ability to execute its maritime strategy. Liu was also known as the father of

---

[88] Ronald O'Rourke, "China Naval Modernization: Implications for U.S. Navy Capabilities — Background and Issues for Congress," CRS Report RL33153 (Washington, DC: Library of Congress, Congressional Research Service, 26 April 2013).

China's aircraft carrier program and he was the most senior and staunch advocate for the acquisition of an aircraft carrier capability.[89] Liu advocated "a medium-sized, conventionally-powered aircraft carrier for limited, air-defense dominated missions," as opposed to large, nuclear powered ones for maritime dominance.[90]

To project power to the southern and eastern fringes of the first island chain, China needed to have portable air power to provide its fleets with adequate air defense. This is especially so in the southern regions of the South China Sea which are beyond the ranges of shore-based aircraft in China yet well within the range of shore-based aircraft of the littoral states that are potential adversaries.[91] Storey and You outlined China's maritime doctrine and the role of aircraft carriers, stating that China's aircraft carrier ambitions grew from the realization that sea control can only be achieved through air superiority.[92] This was especially the case in the South China Sea which stretches up to 950 miles from the Chinese coast, thus well beyond the range of any Chinese fighter aircraft. Apart from power projection, carriers can also be used to support humanitarian and disaster relief operations, and maritime security operations.[93] Thus, the operational need for an aircraft carrier is clear if China intends to exercise effective sea control in the South China Sea and be ready to defend its interests, support operations in the Asia-Pacific and portray itself as a major naval power in the region.

China's need for a carrier capability has thus only increased in the past decade and with the commissioning of the *Liaoning*, China has taken a big stride towards building a naval capability that is aligned with the strategic military goal of achieving sea

---

[89] Nan Li and Christopher Weuve, "China's Aircraft Carrier Ambitions: An Update," *Naval War College Review* 63, no.1(Winter 2010), 13, last assessed 2 June 2013, http://www.usnwc.edu/getattachment/99679d4b-cbc1-4291-933e-a520ea231565/China-s-Aircraft-Carrier-Ambitions--An-Update.

[90] Li, "China's Aircraft Carrier Ambitions: An Update."

[91] The southern tip of the first island chain is more than 1500km from the southern tip of China. Only a fraction of warplanes from the PLAAF and PLNAF have a range of 3000km and even so, would be operating at the limits of their range. Issues of reaction time, mid-air refueling and pilot fatigue would also undermine operational effectiveness at long ranges.

[92] Ian Storey and You Ji, "China's Aircraft Carrier Ambitions: Seeking Truth from Rumors", *Naval War College Review* 57, no.1 (Winter 2004), 75, last accessed 3 June 2013, http://www.usnwc.edu/getattachment/ffc60b3e-d2e6-4142-9b71-6dfa247051f2/

[93] O'Rourke, *China Naval Modernization*, 24.

46

control in the South China Sea. Storey and You assessed in 2004 that China had shelved its carrier plans in deference to more urgent concerns over Taiwan.[94] Since then, the Kuomintang victory in Taiwan's Presidential elections in 2008 and 2012 by the pro-Beijing Ma Ying-jeou has decreased China's apprehensions about Taiwanese agitation for independence; and the South China Sea has returned to be a top foreign policy priority for China. Not only has China pushed ahead with its carrier development, it has also increased its maritime activities in the South China Sea and East China Sea, driving the Western Pacific to the top of its foreign policy agenda.

With the commissioning of its first aircraft carrier *Liaoning* in 2012, China has demonstrated its technical ability to construct and operate a medium sized, conventionally powered aircraft carrier. Although the *Liaoning*'s organic fighter capability is still being built, there is little doubt that China possesses the resources, systems, knowledge and motivation to eventually stand up a fully functional carrier capability.[95]

H.   CONCLUSION

This chapter has outlined the heritage of China's maritime forces and development of the PLAN. Mindful not to let history repeat itself and neglect her strategic maritime interests, China has therefore developed a forward based defensive maritime strategy to protect her mainland and secure her coasts.

It also highlighted China's current maritime strategy, and justifications for its aircraft carrier capability. As the PLAN has grown in size and capability, its reach has also grown to secure China's maritime and economic interests in the region and around the world. In the scheme of China's maritime strategy, the aircraft carrier has a definite strategic role.

By clarifying the strategic coherence and operational requirement of a carrier capability for the PLAN, this chapter lays the foundation for the subsequent chapters where strategic deception concerning the acquisition and development of the *Liaoning* will be examined in detail.

---

[94] Storey and You, "China's Aircraft Carrier Ambitions: Seeking Truth from Rumors," 87.

[95] Storey and You, "China's Aircraft Carrier Ambitions: Seeking Truth from Rumors," 90.

THIS PAGE INTENTIONALLY LEFT BLANK

V. STRATEGIC DECEPTION: EASTERN STRATAGEMS EXPLOIT WESTERN SENSIBILITIES

A. INTRODUCTION

This chapter examines the unique qualities found in Chinese conceptions of strategic deception and its employment as a strategic tool. First, strategic deception as a concept will be contrasted between East and West. Second, we examine Deng Xiaoping's strategic guidance and its application to the *Liaoning* deception. Finally, the Thirty-Six Stratagems from Chinese military history are examined for their relevance to the *Liaoning* deception. This allows us to better unravel China's deception with regards to the *Liaoning* through the lens of Chinese strategic culture concerning deception. References to the peculiar characteristics of Chinese strategic deception in this chapter are specific to the circumstances of the *Liaoning* deception and are thus not exhaustive.

B. WHAT IS STRATEGIC DECEPTION?

In 1981, Heuer defined strategic deception as actions that "aim to manipulate elite perceptions in order to gain competitive advantage. It is usually achieved by passage of information to national or military decision makers either directly or via a nation's intelligence services. Channels for passing such information include public or private statements by government officials, leaks to journalists, double agents and spoofing of technical sensors."[96] While Heuer's 1981 deception is still applicable today, the proliferation of mass media, social media and the internet's associated technologies have certainly increased the vectors for deception and their potential effectiveness.

In this thesis, we examine China's employment of strategic deception to obfuscate its acquisition and development of its first aircraft carrier until the point of no return was passed in its development and a fait accompli was presented to the world. To achieve this, the Chinese executed a strategic deception that not only hoodwinked its own citizens, but other states that may have had an interest in blocking the Chinese from

---

[96] Heuer, "Strategic Deception and Counter-Deception," 294.

acquiring such a capability. What were the unique characteristics of this Chinese strategic deception that allowed it to be successful in our contemporary environment?

C.   CHINESE CONCEPTION OF STRATEGIC DECEPTION

"The Chinese have the oldest (and virtually unbroken) tradition of theory and doctrine on surprise and deception."[97] Among the principles of warfare discussed by Sun Tzu in the first chapter of his treatise on the art of war, he states that soldiers engaged in military warfare should have an endless array of stratagems and ploys to ceaselessly catch the adversary off-guard (兵者，诡道也). This principle has been popularly translated as "all warfare is based on deception" in Western literature.[98]

The idea that one need not necessarily be forthright and be strategically ambiguous so as to leave maximum space for strategic maneuver has long tradition in Chinese culture. Many of these principles are captured in Chinese idioms of expression that are often laden with historical references and meaning. Chinese leaders have used such expressions to guide and inform national strategy. To non-native Chinese speakers, such expressions become a linguistic firewall that is opaque and confusing. It is thus instructive to study the principles behind the face of modern Chinese strategic deception that draw inspiration from Deng's 24 Character strategy and the Thirty-Six Stratagems. Before diving into poetic expressions, it is important to understand China's employment of strategic deception in peacetime.

1.   Strategic Deception in Peace

Western strategic tradition is hardly alien to the concept of strategic deception, having employed deception in warfare throughout history. Examples include Napolean's deceptive campaign maneuvers, Britain's withdrawal from Gallipoli and the Allies' Calais deception for D-day at Normandy.[99] However, Western states have mainly

---

[97] Barton Whaley, *Stratagem: Deception and Surprise in War* (Massachusetts: Artech House, 2007), 42.

[98] Yu, *Sun Tzu on the Art of War*, 51.

[99] Whaley, *Stratagem: Deception and Surprise in War*. Whaley has compiled a comprehensive list deception cases in warfare by mostly western militaries.

limited the use of strategic deception to war and have been less prolific about deception in peace and the interstate competition. In the period leading up to the Second World War, Hitler employed strategic deception to build up his Wehrmacht, influence foreign perceptions of his military strength and conceal Germany's foreign policy goals.[100] Perhaps because it was so successively employed by Hitler, peacetime national strategic deception post Second World War has been ostracized and rarely practiced by Western states. Instead, Western practice of statecraft, diplomacy and governance has been driven by puritan and politically-correct values such as freedom, democracy, honesty and efficiency. Conversely, concepts like deception and propaganda have become associated with dishonesty and ill-intentions—generally frowned upon and best avoided as a policy tool.

Chinese nationalism, on the other hand, was born of a different experience as explained in Chapter II. The war against Japanese aggressors and the civil war between the Communists and Nationalists were marked by strategic deception by both sides before and after hostilities. But peacetime strategic deception had roots in Chinese strategic culture long before the 20th century, and persisted thereafter as well. Chinese history is replete with accounts of statesmen and strategists employing deception to outsmart potential aggressors or achieve strategic advantage - *shi* (势) is a concept regarding one's strategic position or state.[101] Deception has therefore become synonymous with mature statecraft, and the ability to employ strategic deception to achieve national objectives is a quality that endears an astute statesman to his constituents. The achievement of strategic goals through deception is seen as a triumph of superior strategy avoiding the need to resort to war. Therefore, unlike the West that has vilified deception as a peacetime strategic tool, China has embraced deception as a legitimate and powerful strategic tool. Examples of Chinese strategic deception include China's diplomatic deceptions in dealing with the U.S. and Soviet Union at the Treaty of

---

[100] Michael Mihalka, *German Strategic Deception in the 1930s*, RAND Corporation (Santa Monica: RAND, 1980), 7.

[101] Kissinger, *On China*, 31.

Versailles[102], the involvement of Chinese "volunteers" in the 1950 Korean War[103], and the investments in U.S. securities made by China's sovereign wealth fund.[104] Two significant non-Chinese but still Eastern examples of strategic deception against the West come to mind: Japan's foreign policy deception against the U.S. leading up to the 1941 Pearl Harbor attack and North Korea's deception before its attack on South Korea in 1950.[105]

The most celebrated strategists and statesmen in Chinese history were less warriors than crafty strategists. These wise counsels excelled through sharpness of mind —using guile and deception to defeat foes who relied on superior military strength. Among the most well-known are the deceptive exploits of military strategists like *Wei* (魏) kingdom's *Xun Yu* (旬余), *Wu* (吴) kingdom's *Zhou Yu* (周瑜) and *Shu* (蜀) kingdom's *Zhuge Liang* (诸葛亮) of the Three Kingdoms era. These exploits are still celebrated in Chinese literature and popular culture. The wisest Chinese rulers were those who had in their employment shrewd strategists who could win battles without the need to be fight. The legacies of Marshal Peng Dehuai (彭德怀) in the PLA and Admiral Liu Huaqing (刘华清) in shaping the PLAN and China's maritime strategy are more recent examples.

In Chinese imperial bureaucracies, a Chinese ruler and his strategist ranked above his civilian *wen* (文) and military *wu* (武) courtiers, thus both military and non-military policies were subsets of a larger national strategy. This unity of command and civilian control over the military was a result of generations of emphasis on the primacy of intellectual progress (through Confucian teachings and imperial examinations) and

---

102 Bruce A. Elleman, *Diplomacy and Deception: The Secret History of Sino-Soviet Diplomatic Relations, 1917-1927* (Armonk, New York: M.E. Sharpe, 1997), 19.

103 Max Hastings, *The Korean War* (New York: Simon and Schuster, 1987), 130.

104 Eric. C. Anderson and Jeffrey G. Engstrom, *China's Use of Perception Management and Strategic Deception*, U.S.-China Economic and Security Review Commission, November 2009, http://www.uscc.gov/Research/china%E2%80%99s-use-perception-management-and-strategic-deception, 39.

105 *Attack on Pearl Harbor 1941: Conclusions of the U.S. Congressional Committee, 1946* (London: Stationary Office, 2001), 25

enlightened civilian policies.[106] War as a policy outcome became a choice of last resort and an indication that civilian policy had failed.[107] The employment of strategic deception in civilian policy in peacetime was therefore considered a viable strategy to avoid war and achieve strategic gains that would delay or render war unnecessary.

Although communist China has distanced itself from its imperial past, the intellectual heritage of employing strategic deception in peacetime lived on its literature and culture. Mao was known to have studied the Chinese classics including the Romance of the Three Kingdoms and handily quoted strategy and tactics from its stories. Drawing on the rich Chinese historical literature, Mao's generals even used the strategic alliance of *Shu* and *Wu* kingdoms against the powerful *Wei* kingdom in the Three Kingdoms era as a conceptual comparison for their own deliberations about China's alliance strategy with the Soviet Union and the U.S.[108]

Figure 3 compares various aspects of the Three Kingdoms era and modern day China, looking specifically at the rulers, principal strategists and the strategies of each kingdom. The Wei kingdom controlled Northern China and was in possession of abundant resources and troops. Thus its strategy was to use its superior force against the Shu and Wu kingdoms. Wei ruler Cao Cao recognized talents and recruited them using material rewards. Shu kingdom occupied China's Southern interior and was militarily inferior to Wei. Thus it sought an alliance with the Wu kingdom against Wei. However, Shu's Liu Bei was assisted by the extremely capable talent strategist Zhuge Liang and generals whom he recruited with his sincerity and altruistic cause of restoring the Han dynasty. The Wu kingdom occupied the riverine and mountainous southern coastal region. Similar to Shu kingdom, its military force was weaker than Wei's but unlike Shu, its geography made it easily to defend and repel Wei. Thus Wu was quite content to remain isolated from both even though Shu constantly broached an alliance with Wu. The Wu kingdom was matriarchal so family and community ties were strong. Its talents

---

[106] John K. Fairbank, *Chinese Ways in Warfare* (Massachusetts: Harvard University Press, 1974), 4.

[107] Fairbank, *Chinese Ways in Warfare*, 7.

[108] Kissinger, *On China*, 211.

and generals came mainly from its own community and many were skilled in maritime warfare on the rivers and lakes that dominated Wu terrain. Contrasting all this with modern day China, Xi Jinping reigns as the de facto leader of the Communist state. His strategists in military affairs are likely to come from the Central Military Commission members. China's military today is moving away from the preponderance of numerical superiority and toward modern technology and methods. Talented people in the military service can be recruited and are convinced of their cause as a result of nationalistic communist machinery that pervades Chinese society at all levels. Today's China strives towards the "China Dream," seeking both material and spiritual wealth as the national utopia.

Comparison of Three Kingdoms and People's Republic of China: Rulers, Strategists & Strategy

Wei Kingdom	Shu Kingdom	Wu Kingdom	PRC 2013
Ruler	Ruler	Ruler	CCP Leader
Cao Cao	Liu Bei	Sun Ce	Xi Jinping
		Sun Quan	
Strategist	Strategist	Strategist	Strategist
Xun Yu	Zhuge Liang	Zhou Yu	CMC Members?
Guo Jia	Pang Tong	Lu Su	
Strategy	Strategy	Strategy	Strategy
Superior Force	Alliance with Wu	Exploit Geography	Modern Force
Exploit Talents	Cultivate Talents	Raise Talents	Cultivate Talents
Material Rewards	Principles & Values	Family & Community	China Dream

Figure 3.   Comparison of Chinese Rulers, Strategists, Strategies

The propensity for China to employ strategic deception in peacetime is therefore accessed to be likely based on its historical behavior as well as its strategic culture. The following two sections highlight the principles that serve as vehicles for the application of Chinese strategic deception.

2. Deng Xiaoping's "24 Character" Strategy

A 2008 Office of Secretary of Defense (OSD) report on the Military Power of China referred to Deng Xiaoping's "24 Character" strategy which the Chinese leader developed in 1991. The 24 characters were from Deng's famous guidance that consisted of six four-word idioms: '冷静观察, 站稳脚跟, 沉着应付, 韬光养晦, 善于守拙, 绝不当头.'[109] The OSD translated each four-word phrase in the six phrases to mean "observe calmly; secure our position; cope with affairs calmly; hide our capacities and bide our time; be good at maintaining a low profile; and never claim leadership."[110] It also reported that "taken as a whole, the "24 Character" strategy remains instructive in that it suggests a strategy to maximize future options through avoiding unnecessary provocations, shunning excessive international burdens, and building up China's power over a long-term."[111] The OSD also stated Deng's strategy has endured beyond his tenure and continues to be a part of China's strategic psyche.[112] The "24 Character" strategy succinctly summarizes the core principles driving Chinese strategic deception. Of particular interest to us is the fourth phrase, "韬光养晦", which when read in conjunction with the fifth "善于守拙" and sixth "绝不当头" phrases collectively advices the nation to hide and bide, observe with strategic patience and keep a low profile. These strategic actions are synergistic and mutually reinforcing.

The Chinese idiom"韬光养晦" conveys the intention to hide one's own capacities and bide one's time for an opportune moment. It is often used in situations where one's adversary is stronger and one requires sufficient time to build capabilities that can deal with the opponent and then shift the strategic situation to one's own advantage at an opportune moment. This strategy requires more than just the cultivation of strategic patience. In Chinese literature, it includes the grudging acceptance of humiliation by a stronger adversary until one is ready and the time is right. While the stronger adversary

---

[109] Office of the Secretary of Defense, *Military Power of the People's Republic of China 2008, last assessed 4 June 2013,* http://www.defense.gov/pubs/pdfs/China_Military_Report_08.pdf.

[110] OSD, *Military Power of the People's Republic of China 2008,* 8.

[111] OSD, *Military Power of the People's Republic of China 2008,* 8.

[112] OSD, *Military Power of the People's Republic of China 2008,* 8.

gloats in his domination, the weaker army betrays a posture of weakness and quietly builds his strength. Sun Tzu makes a similar observation in the *Art of War*: "Therefore, when capable, feign incapacity; when active, inactivity."[113]

China has operationalized this hide and bide strategy in its *Liaoning* deception. First, even though China today has the largest Asian Navy in terms of numbers major combatants, it is still a long way from catching up with the U.S. Navy in terms of its ability to project power offshore.[114] Throughout the late 1990s and the first decade of the new millennium when the *Liaoning* was being developed, the state of the PLAN was even worse. Thus, the PLAN saw itself occupying a position of weakness against the U.S. Navy. This relative weakness of the PLAN was capitalized upon by the U.S. in 1996 when the U.S. deployed its carrier battle groups near the Taiwan Straits following tensions brought on by Chinese missile tests aimed at intimidating Taiwan.[115]

Second, while China acquired and developed its aircraft carrier, it continued to insist that it was merely studying the capability and had no plans to construct one. In acquiring the *Varyag*, it insisted that the rusting hulk was meant to be a floating casino in Macau. Even when China first acknowledged constructing a carrier in 2011, the PLAN made no bold claims about its capabilities or function. When the *Liaoning* was commissioned in 2012, the PLAN merely stated that it was for research and training.[116] These understated comments were designed to portray the aircraft carrier *Liaoning* in non-threatening light and to create the perception that it posed little or no threat to the region.

Third, China bided its time in not officially acknowledging the carrier until 2011 because it wanted to delay an acknowledgement for as long as practically possible to prevent any foreign obstructions to the development of its first aircraft carrier. It is

---

[113] Yu, *Sun Tzu on the Art of War*, 51. Sun Tzu's saying in Chinese: "故能而示为不能，用而示之不用。"

[114] Office of the Secretary of Defense, *Military Power of the People's Republic of China 2013*, last accessed 4 June 2013, http://www.defense.gov/pubs/2013_China_Report_FINAL.pdf.

[115] Brian Nolton, "Second Carrier is sent by U.S. as 'precaution': Beijing warns the U.S. on Taiwan Intervention," *New York Times*, 12 March 1996, http://www.nytimes.com/1996/03/12/news/12iht-pent.t.html.

[116] "China's first aircraft carrier commissioned," *Xinhua* (China).

highly possible that by 2011, the development of the carrier had already passed the point of no return and the critical technologies and systems required were already completed.

Chinese behavior regarding the *Liaoning* acquisition and development was a classical exhibition of the hide and bide strategy, and manifestation of Deng's "24 Character" strategy.

3.   The Thirty-Six Stratagems[117]

Many Chinese historical accounts have been condensed into idioms of expression that convey the narrative core of the stratagem in achieving an objective. The Thirty-Six Stratagems (三十六计) commonly found in Chinese literature and referred to in its military history are examples of such idioms. The Thirty-Six Stratagems, like many other ancient Chinese literary artifacts, are difficult to attribute to a single source. Thirty-six is the product of 'six and six'—which in the Chinese linguistic tradition is used as a prop to simply mean 'numerous.' Current understanding of the Thirty-Six Stratagems come from 20th century popular literature, especially by Chinese Communist Party newspapers.[118] The Thirty-Six Stratagems are organized into six chapters of six stratagems. Each chapter relates to a specific strategic situation for stratagem employment. The six chapters are:

- Chapter 1(胜战计): Stratagems employed when in a strategically advantageous posture (绝对优势)

- Chapter 2(敌战计): Stratagems employed when one's strategically posture is equal to the enemy (势均力敌态势)

- Chapter 3 (攻战计): Stratagems employed when in an offensive strategic posture (进攻态势)

- Chapter 4 (混战计): Stratagems employed when in a chaotic strategic posture (军阀混战态势)

- Chapter 5 (并战计): Stratagems employed when in a strategically ambiguous posture (友军反为敌态势)

---

117 See Appendix 1: 36 Stratagems from Chinese History, for the full list and translation of the 36 Stratagems.

118 "三十六计初探" [Exploring the Thirty-Six Stratagems], *中国谋略科学网*[Chinese Strategic Science Network], last accessed 4 June 2013, http://www.szbf.net/Article_Show.asp?ArticleID=1490.

- Chapter 6 (败战计): Stratagems employed when in a disadvantageous strategic posture (败军态势)

The following section will explain selected stratagems employed in deception that shed light on the *Liaoning* deception.

Stratagem 1: Man Tian Guo Hai (瞒天过海): "Crossing the Oceans without Heaven's Knowledge"[119]

The translation has two implied meanings: (1) Those who believe they have taken ample precautions are liable to be caught off guard. (2) Familiarity breeds desensitization and lowers arousal of suspicions.

In the case of the *Liaoning* deception, the rusting hulk of the *Varyag* literally crossed the oceans under the noses and scrutiny of the surveillance satellites in the heavens as it sailed from the Black Sea to China. Closer to the intended meaning of the term, by the time the *Varyag* was on its way to China after substantial delay in the Black Sea, world media was no longer interested in its voyage and other world events had taken precedence. This was a result of China's cover story for the purchase of the *Varyag* that deflected unnecessary attention from the media. The unforeseen almost year long delay that the ship encountered in exiting the Black Sea through the Bosphorus Straits also lessened media attention. Combined, these events led to little media scrutiny about the *Varyag*'s journey. Thus, the *Varyag* was able to complete its voyage with little undue attention or obstruction.

Stratagem 5: Cheng Huo Da Jie (趁火打劫): "Loot a Burning House"[120]

When the enemy suffers a major crisis, seize the chance to gain advantage. In the *Liaoning* deception, China was fortunate that the attention and resources of the U.S. were fully engaged in Iraq and Afghanistan from 2001 onwards. This allowed for much of the *Liaoning*'s development to proceed without undue scrutiny and interference from the U.S. While China may not have been complicit in the events leading up to the U.S. campaigns, China capitalized on U.S. distractions in Central Asia to maximize its own strategic gains.

---

[119] Sun, *The Wiles of War: 36 Military Strategies From Ancient China*, 1.

[120] Sun, *The Wiles of War: 36 Military Strategies From Ancient China*, 43.

Stratagem 7: Wu Zhong Sheng You (无中生有): "Create Something Out of Nothing"[121]

To make a deliberate false move and to transform it into a genuine one after the enemy has been convinced of its falsity. The false move that China made was to state that the *Varyag* would not be refurbished into an operational carrier. It was allegedly to have been a floating casino in Macau and this was China's position despite contradicting reports about the lack of sufficient depth of water in Macau and the Macau government's own ignorance. Eventually, the idea that the *Varyag* would be anything but an operational carrier was accepted as the convenient truth by the broader media. Western intelligence reported that the difficulties involved in converting the rusting *Varyag* hulk into an aircraft carrier were too complex to be overcome and China did nothing to contradict such reporting. The false move having been believed, China spent more than a decade of work rebuilding the *Varyag* which was re-launched in 2012 as the PLAN's first aircraft carrier *Liaoning*.

Stratagem 10: Xiao Li Cang Dao (笑里藏刀): "Conceal a Dagger Behind a Smile"[122]

Reassure the adversary to cause him to be complacent while working in secret to subdue him. Alternatively, to prepare in secret before taking decisive action to preclude the enemy any opportunity to change his position. The *Varyag* was being refurbished in secret for a decade, during that time China gave multiple reassurances that no carrier construction was underway, allaying the concerns of regional countries. When it was finally revealed in 2011 that the *Varyag* was being made into an operational carrier, a *fait accompli* by China had already been accomplished.

Stratagem 14: Jie Shi Huan Hun (借尸还魂): "To Revive A Corpse"[123]

Advocates the masterful use of the apparently useless in order to achieve a goal without the adversary's suspicion. The *Varyag* was originally literally a corpse of a ship—gutted of its organs and left to rust in disrepair. China purchased the corpse of the *Varyag* at three times its scrap value and reincarnated it as the *Liaoning* after a decade of

---

[121] Sun, *The Wiles of War: 36 Military Strategies From Ancient China*, 60.

[122] Sun, *The Wiles of War: 36 Military Strategies From Ancient China*, 88.

[123] Sun, *The Wiles of War: 36 Military Strategies From Ancient China*, 125.

refurbishment—much to the surprise of experts who thought the task was above China's capabilities or simply not worth the effort and resources required.

Stratagem 20: Hun Shui Mo Yu (混水摸鱼): "Catch a Fish in Muddled Waters"[124]

Take advantage of an adversary's difficult situation and exploit his weaknesses and lack of judgment. If the *Varyag* was the fish, the muddled waters would be the chaotic international environment after the September 11 attacks, including the decade long U.S. campaigns in Iraq and Afghanistan that were a major distraction of U.S. attention away from East Asia and the Asia Pacific region. China therefore caught its carrier "fish" in the muddled waters of the Global War on Terror, among other "fish" that it also netted during America's decade lost to two voluntary wars.

Stratagem 21: Jin Chan Tuo Qiao (金蝉脱壳): "The Cicada Sloughs its Skin"[125]

Maintaining the appearance of inaction while in fact, taking action in secret. In sloughing its skin, the cicada leaves behind a shell of apparent inaction to deceive the predator when it has in fact fled. In its statements regarding the development and refurbishment of the *Varyag*, China maintained a line of apparent inaction towards its hidden objectives until very late in the development of the aircraft carrier *Liaoning*.

Stratagem 27: Jia Chi Bu Dian (假痴不癫): Feign Foolishness even if not Insane.[126]

Feign foolish ignorance and inaction to hide your intentions while allowing the enemy to believe you to be foolish and therefore lower his guard. In developing the *Varyag*, China never claimed any ability to do so nor did it contradict foreign assessments about its apparent inability to refurbish *Varyag* into a functional carrier. By feigning apparent inability and passively encouraging pessimistic projections of its capability, China achieved its strategic objective of building the *Liaoning* with minimal interference.

Stratagem 29: Shu Sang Kai Hua (树上开花): To Make a Tree Blossom[127]

---

124 Sun, *The Wiles of War: 36 Military Strategies From Ancient China*, 178.

125 Sun, *The Wiles of War: 36 Military Strategies From Ancient China*, 189.

126 Sun, *The Wiles of War: 36 Military Strategies From Ancient China*, 242.

Exploit external appearances to create an advantageous situation. One can obscure the truth by creating an illusion that the enemy believes in. In *Liaoning*'s case, the conversion of the other two carriers that China acquired into entertainment facilities perpetuated the belief that the *Varyag* would be similarly converted. This obscured the true purpose of the *Varyag*'s acquisition for development into an operational carrier.

Stratagem 32: Kong Cheng Ji (空城计): Empty City Stratagem[128]

Bear a confident outward appearance when in a weak position to give the impression of strength and sow doubt in a stronger adversary about the true nature of your strength. While China lacked an aircraft carrier (a weakness), it developed and demonstrated other weapons systems like the anti-satellite missile and anti-ship cruise missile to give the impression that it was self-confident in its own abilities and nonchalant about U.S. military strength. It also gave the impression that there was no urgency to develop her own aircraft carrier.

While we have no direct knowledge about China's employment of the stratagems in a conscious and deliberate manner, we can use our understanding of the stratagems and examine the *Liaoning* deception from that perspective. Such explanations also help non-Chinese scholars understand what could be going through Chinese minds in their strategic conception of situations.

D.   CONCLUSION

Chinese deception has a rich and long history that has been captured in Chinese cultural consciousness and popular literature. While Western martial and political culture has employed strategic deception before, its employment in today's politically correct and ethically constrained Western societies is stymied. This contrasts with China's sophisticated and nuanced employment of strategic deception in many spheres of national interest. Deng's 24 Character strategy and the Thirty-Six Stratagems were used as platforms to analyze the *Liaoning* deception. While it is unclear how China exactly employed the Chinese civilization's collective experience and knowledge of

---

[127] Sun, *The Wiles of War: 36 Military Strategies From Ancient China*, 261.

[128] Sun, *The Wiles of War: 36 Military Strategies From Ancient China*, 296.

strategic deception, sufficient evidence exists for the reconstruction of events and application of known deception concepts to the events. The Chinese perspective on strategic deception provided in this chapter will serve as a useful platform for comparison with a Western method of analyzing deception utilizing Heuer's Theory of Competing Hypothesis examined in the Chapter VII.

VI.   THE *LIAONING* DECEPTION: "CROSSING THE OCEAN WITHOUT HEAVEN'S KNOWLEDGE"

A.   INTRODUCTION

In September 2012, China commissioned the *Liaoning* into the People's Liberation Army Navy (PLAN). She was China's first aircraft carrier and was built based on the former USSR's Admiral Kutznetsov class multi-role carrier design[129]. To many observers, this marked a significant Chinese stride towards the development of its blue-water naval capability that would allow the PLAN to better project its power and influence in maritime East Asia.[130]

The commissioning of China's first carrier should have come as no surprise as its procurement, construction and development were constantly followed by defense and intelligence agencies internationally since a Macau-based Chinese company first bought the de-activated hull from Ukraine in 1998.[131] However, the fruition of China's initial carrier development constituted a coup for China for the following reasons: the development of a significant naval capability; proving detractors about its military capabilities wrong; showcasing its naval and shipbuilding capabilities; and strengthening its credentials as a shrewd strategic player. This chapter posits that the commissioning of the *Liaoning* was a masterful coup by China and a strategic surprise to its detractors. As late as 2009, U.S. Department of Defense (DOD) estimated that China's carrier capability would not be realized before 2015.[132]

---

[129] James Hardy and Poornima Subramaniam, "China Commissions First Aircraft Carrier," *Jane's Navy International*, 25 September 2012.

[130] O'Rourke, Ronald. *China Naval Modernization: Implications for U.S. Navy Capabilities – Background and Issues for Congress.* CRS Report RL33153. Washington, DC: Library of Congress, Congressional Research Service, 26 April 2013, 19.

[131] Glenn Scholss and Adam Lee, "Mystery Macau company buys aircraft carrier," *South China Morning Post*, 19 March 1998.

[132] "Chinese aircraft carrier capability unlikely before 2015, says U.S. report," *Jane's Navy International*, 31 Mar 2009.

The commissioning of the aircraft carrier was a significant event on both the domestic and international fronts for China. International media outlets outside China gave the *Liaoning*'s commissioning more than its fair share of coverage expressing a spectrum of opinions ranging from grudging respect and concern for Chinese military modernization to dismissals about the operational inadequacy of a single carrier and the lingering requirement for China to build a credible carrier air capability.

This chapter investigates Chinese use of strategic military deception in building its nascent carrier capability and argues that China successfully employed deception to achieve a significant milestone towards the development of its carrier capability. The chapter will begin with an examination of the timeline of the *Liaoning*'s acquisition and development. This is followed by an examination of reports concerning the building of China's aircraft carrier capability during the period that the *Liaoning* was being refurbished. The discrepancies between the *Liaoning*'s actual refurbishment and China's official position on aircraft carrier development will lead to the explanation of a plausible deception ploy in the development of the *Liaoning*. The final phase of analysis proposes various measures employed by China to manage the *Liaoning* deception.

B. CHINESE AIRCRAFT CARRIER LIAONING: ACQUISITION AND DEVELOPMENT

This section covers the acquisition and development of the *Liaoning*. There are numerous websites and articles that have detailed the process of *Liaoning*'s transformation. This section simply provides a brief summary of the main developmental milestones of the *Liaoning* and lays the foundation for the analysis of the deception that will be discussed in the later part of this chapter.

The *Liaoning* began life as the ex-Soviet Admiral Kuznetsov class aircraft carrier *Varyag* that was launched in 1985 and was structurally complete but without any systems when construction ceased in 1992. Ownership was transferred to Ukraine after the USSR broke up and the unfinished carrier was initially put up for sale in 1992. China was reportedly on the verge of completing the transfer with the Ukrainian government when the deal fell apart.[133]   By 1998 the rusting hulk was put up for sale again. This time, the Macau-based private travel agency Chong Lot won the auction for the hulk with a US$20 million bid that was triple its scrap value.[134] From the Black Sea, the *Varyag* took four years to reach the Chinese port of Dalian in 2002. The *Varyag* was stuck in the Black Sea for more than 15 months because Turkey had declined to allow what it deemed as a navigational-hazard through the Bosphorous Straits.[135] This impasse was only resolved when the China's Deputy Foreign Minister intervened in 2001 and made promises of economic aid to Turkey in exchange for the *Varyag*'s passage.[136] From 2002 to 2004, there was very little official news about the *Varyag*. However, satellite pictures showed that work had already begun on refurbishing the *Varyag* in dry dock during this time.[137] It is surmised that a decision on the *Varyag*'s long term development was also made in China during this time because after 2004, the development of the *Varyag* rapidly ramped up. By 2005, *Jane's* reported that the *Varyag* was being repainted in a naval paint scheme and suggested that it was *not* going to be an entertainment facility in Macau.[138] In 2006, U.S. and Taiwan analysts surmised that the *Varyag* would be refurbished as an operational carrier for training, however China continued to dismiss any claims that suggest a military function for the *Varyag*.[139] In 2007, the U.S. DOD reported that the *Varyag* was undergoing extensive refurbishment but was still unsure about when China could actually field an operational carrier. By 2009, the *Varyag* was towed to a larger dry dock in Dalian where it was assessed to have been fitted with major machinery and systems.[140] During the next year, weapon systems were installed and in 2011, China

---

[133] "China not planning to buy aircraft carrier from Ukraine," *Kyodo News Service*, 12 October 1992.

[134] Glenn Scholss and Adam Lee, "Mystery Macau company buys aircraft carrier."

[135] Storey and You, "China's Aircraft Carrier Ambitions: Seeking Truth from Rumors," 82.

[136] Storey and You, "China's Aircraft Carrier Ambitions: Seeking Truth from Rumors," 83.

[137] "Varyag's transformation into an operational aircraft carrier," *The Rising Sea Dragon in Asia*, accessed 21 May 2013, http://www.jeffhead.com/redseadragon/varyagtransform.htm.

[138] "Is China building a carrier?" *Jane's Defence Weekly*, 11 August 2005.

[139] David Lague, "Do China's strategic ambitions include a carrier?" *The International Herald Tribune*, 31 January 2006.

[140] "China continues development of an aircraft carrier," *Jane's Country Risk Daily Report*, 27 May 2009.

officially confirmed that it was building an aircraft carrier.[141] In September 2012, after 12 months of extensive sea trials, the *Varyag* was officially commissioned into the PLAN as the *Liaoning* in a symbolic ceremony attended by the highest levels of China's leadership. Table 5 below summarizes the events directly related to the *Varyag*'s transformation into the *Liaoning*.

The metamorphosis of the *Varyag* from a rusting hulk to the pride of the PLAN was an engineering and publicity coup for China. China proved detractors who said that it would not be feasible or prohibitively expensive wrong. Additionally, the success of the *Liaoning* showed that China exceeded the capabilities with regard to what other countries thought it could achieve. The refurbishment of the *Varyag* was also accomplished in a relatively short time, surpassing most foreign estimates of how long it would take. The *Varyag*'s transformation suggests not just quality technical resources and skills but also elaborate and effective planning and execution by China's military industrial complex. Keeping this in mind, the next section examines China's public positions about the *Varyag*'s transformation and carrier development during the same period as the *Varyag*'s refurbishment.

Table 5.   Events Directly Related to China's Transformation of the Aircraft Carrier *Varyag* into the *Liaoning*

Year	Events
1988	Original carrier was launched as the Riga by Soviet Navy in 1988. Renamed *Varyag* in 1998.
1992	August. China reputed to be interested in initial sale of *Varyag* through official channels.[1] October. China says not planning to buy *Varyag* from Ukraine.[2]
1998	March. Purchase of the *Varyag* hulk for US$20 million by Macau-based private company Chong Lot for conversion to a floating casino.[3]
2000	From June and for the next 15 months, the *Varyag* is stuck in the Black Sea because Turkey refuses to allow passage through Bosphorus Straits due to safety concerns.
Continued on next page.	

---

[141] Yinan Hu, Xiaokun Li and Haipei Cui, "Official confirms China building aircraft carrier," *China Daily,* 12 July 2011, accessed 21 May 2013, http://www.chinadaily.com.cn/china/2011-07/12/content_12881089.htm.

2001	<u>September</u>. Turkey calls for $1 billion guarantee for passage through Bosphorus.[4] <u>November</u>. Turkey relents to allow passage through Bosphorus Strait after protracted negotiations with Chinese government acting on behalf of Macau company Chong Lot. China reportedly offered $360 million in economic aid to Turkey. The *Varyag* rounds Cape of Good Hope enroute to China.
2002	<u>February</u>. Macau company Chong Lot is not granted casino license by Macau authorities, harbor in Macau also assessed to be too shallow for the *Varyag*.[5] China insists the *Varyag* is designated to be a floating casino. <u>March</u>. The *Varyag* finally enters Chinese naval port of Dalian after completing 4-year journey from Ukraine.[6]
2003-2004	<u>March</u>. China employs retired Ukrainian admiral as a tour guide for the *Varyag*.[7] Little news about the *Varyag*. Assessed to be an important period as it was likely during this period that a decision was made by the Chinese government to develop the *Varyag* into a functional carrier if it had not been already made prior. Ownership of the *Varyag* was likely transferred from Chong Lot to the Chinese government during this period.
2005	<u>August</u>. *Jane's* reports that the *Varyag* has been repainted in military colors and being refurbished in Dalian. Chong Lot's casino claim discredited.[8] Satellite photos show extensive preparation of deck and superstructure for possible flight operations. China reported to be repairing the *Varyag*.[9]
2006	U.S. and Taiwan analysts assess the *Varyag* is to be rebuilt as a carrier for training. PLA denies claims.[10]
2007	Refurbishment and outfitting of the *Varyag* reported by U.S Department of Defence.[11]
2009	The *Varyag* is moved to another dry dock for suspected installation of engines and heavy equipment. *Janes* reports the *Varyag* moved to new Dalian drydock and activities consistent with refurbishment of the ship.[12]
2011	<u>June</u>. Chief General Staff of PLA officially acknowledges that China is building an aircraft carrier for first time.[13] <u>August</u>. *Varyag* begins sea trials.[14]
2012	<u>August</u>. *Varyag* sea trials reported completed. <u>September</u>. *Varyag* handed over to PLAN. Commissioned as *Liaoning*.

ources:

[1] "Secret Chinese report on purchase of Ukrainian aircraft carrier," *Kyodo News Service*, 14 August 1992.

[2] "China not planning to buy aircraft carrier from Ukraine," *BBC Summary of World Broadcasts*, 12 October 1992.

[3] Glenn Schloss, "Macau company to convert aircraft carrier into 600m floating palace; $1.6b hotel plan for warship," *South China Morning Post*, 11 November 1998, 3.

[4] "Turkey calls for more guarantees over Varyag," *Jane's Defence Weekly*, 14 September 2001.

[5] "Soviet carriers find a new home in China," *Jane's Intelligence Review*, 21 March 2002.

Continued on next page.

Continued from previous page

[6] Ian Storey, "Soviet aircraft carriers find a new home in China," *Jane's Intelligence Review*, 21 March 2002.

[7] "China employs retired Ukrainian admiral," *BBC Summary of World Broadcasts*, 11 March 2003.

[8] "Is China building a carrier?" *Jane's Defence Weekly*, 11 August 2005.

[9] "Chinese navy repairing unfinished Ukrainian aircraft carrier Varyag," *Zhongguo Tongxun She* 中国通讯社 (Hong Kong), 16 August 2005.

[10] David Lague, "Do China's strategic ambitions include a carrier?" *The International Herald Tribune*, 31 January 2006.

[11] "China's naval ambitions: Congressional report details major warship programmes," *Jane's Navy International*, 20 June 2007.

[12] "China continues development of an aircraft carrier," *Jane's Country Risk Daily Report*, 27 May 2009.

[13] Yinan Hu, Xiaokun Li and Haipei Cui, "Official confirms China building aircraft carrier," *China Daily,* 12 July 2011, http://www.chinadaily.com.cn/china/2011-07/12/content_12881089.htm.

[14] "U.S. Satellite pictures China aircraft carrier Varyag," *BBC News*, 14 December 2011, http://www.bbc.co.uk/news/world-asia-16190926.

C. DISPARITY BETWEEN CHINA'S POSITIONS ON AIRCRAFT CARRIER DEVELOPMENT AND REALITY

This section examines China's position on the issue of aircraft carrier development and contrasts it with the reality of known developments with the *Varyag* and associated capabilities. The intent of this comparison is to highlight the difference between China's official positions and the reality of actual developments so that the depth and magnitude of China's deception is apparent.

An examination of China's positions from 1998 to 2011 reflected a picture of consistent official denial about any carrier construction and the *Varyag*'s refurbishment. However, there were occasional statements by PLA officials about the viability of aircraft carriers for China as well as speculative dates about when China may unveil its carrier capability. Table 6 below summarizes the events relating to China's aircraft carrier development as well as China's stated positions on the issue.

Table 6.   Events relating to China's Aircraft Carrier Development

Year	Events
1993	June. Hong Kong journal reports about China's apparent urgency to build aircraft carriers.[1]
1997	January. Hong Kong paper reports about China's "two craft" plans to build an aircraft carrier by 2000. Alleges Chinese Communist Party Central Committee has advanced building plans by 5 years.[2]
1998	March. Macau based company purchases *Varyag* for three times the scrap value. Media reports that it will be converted into a floating hotel based at Macau.[3] China makes no official comment.
2000	January. Hong Kong paper reports China embarking on plans to build first carrier.[4] PLA debunks foreign reports about China's carrier plans and insists carriers are outside China's national strategy.[5]
2002	March. *Jane's* reports that China's carrier plans are stalled due to more pressing national priorities and postulates that refurbishing *Varyag* would be prohibitively expensive.[6]
2004	Speculation by independent observers that China will build three carriers by 2010.[7]
2005	China reported to be repairing *Varyag*.[8]
2006	January. *International Herald Tribune* reports China's aircraft carrier construction underway. China denies any construction.[9] October. PLA General Armament Department Vice Chairman states China's study of carrier construction and indispensability of carriers in protecting maritime interests.[10]
2007	March. PLA claims China may have aircraft carrier by 2010.[11] April. PLA debunks Chinese aircraft carrier threat theory with *Kiev* and *Minsk* as examples.[12] May. Commander U.S. Pacific Fleet confirms China's interest in carriers after official visit to the country.[13] November. Korean paper reports Chinese nuclear-powered carrier scheduled to be completed by 2020. Also reports Shanghai shipyard capable of handling 30,000 ton class vessel. Reports Chinese interest in $2.5 billion purchase of 50 Su-33 aircraft from Russia.[14]
2008	September. Jane's reports PLAN naval aviators begin training. Also reports earliest carrier flight training in 2010.[15] November. China's Ministry of National Defense's Foreign Affairs Office director states that having carrier is dream of any great power and question is not whether one possesses carrier but what one does with it.[16] PLA denies carrier construction in progress but does not preclude future carrier capability.[17]

Continued on next page.

	Continued from previous page **December.** China's Ministry of National Defense states that China is seriously considering adding aircraft carriers to its fleet because the carrier is a symbol of a country's national strength and the competitiveness of it naval force.[18] China uses deployment of counter-piracy naval task force to Somalia to develop and project its forces. A precursor to carrier deployment?[19]
2009	**January.** HK paper reports China expected to announce carrier project at 60th anniversary of PRC.[20] Also reports Chinese plans to deploy carriers to South China Sea to protect SLOCs and territories. **March.** U.S. D.O.D reports to Congress that China's carrier ambitions unlikely to be realized before 2015.[21] *Jane's* reports PLAN program to train 50 navy pilots for fixed-wing operations on carriers. **April.** CCP paper justifies aircraft carrier capability.[22] Wuhan Naval Research Lab observed to have full logistics training deck and aircraft carrier island mock-up for training.[23]
2011	**January.** HK business fails in attempt to buy the United Kingdom's HMS Invincible for scrap.[24] **July.** China's Ministry of Defence confirms that first aircraft carrier will be ready and says it would not be for combat missions but for training.[25]
2012	**August.** *Varyag*'s tenth and final sea trial completed.[26] **September.** *Varyag* handed over to PLAN. Commissioned as *Liaoning*.

Sources:

[1] "Urgency of building aircraft carriers," *Tangtai* (Hong Kong), No. 26, 15 May 1993, 74-77.

[2] "China to produce first aircraft carrier by the year 2000," *Ping Kuo Jih Pao*苹果日报 [Apple Daily] (Hong Kong), 4 January 1997, A14.

[3] Glenn Schloss, "Macau company to convert aircraft carrier into 600m floating palace; $1.6b hotel plan for warship," *South China Morning Post*, 11 November 1998.

[4] "China to build first aircraft carrier," *Ming Pao*明报 (Hong Kong) , 12 January 2000, A15.

[5] "Hong Kong paper dismisses report on plan to build aircraft carrier," *Ta Kung Pao* (Hong Kong), 15 January 2000.

[6] Ian Storey and You Ji, "Chinese aspirations to acquire aircraft-carrier capability stall," *Jane's Intelligence Review*, 21 March 2002.

[7] Anthony Paul, "The great Chinese aircraft carrier mystery," *The Straits Times* (Singapore), 30 March 2004.

[8] "Chinese navy repairing unfinished Ukrainian aircraft carrier Varyag," *Zhongguo Tongxun She* 中国通讯社 (Hong Kong), 16 August 2005.

[9] David Lague, "Do China's strategic ambitions include a carrier?" *The International Herald Tribune*, 31 Jan 2006.

[10] "China's naval ambitions: Congressional report details major warship programs," *Jane's Navy International*, 20 June 2007.

[11] "Chinese Admiral says China may have aircraft carrier by 2010," *Wen Wei Po*文汇报 (Hong Kong), 7 March 2007.

Continued on next page.

Continued from previous page.

[12] Kung-pai Chuang, "Chinese Navy Expert refutes 'Aircraft Carrier Threat' Theory," *Zhongguo Tongxun She* 中国通讯社 (Hong Kong), 26 April 2007.

[13] Richard Halloran and Bill Gertz, "China intent on aircraft carrier goal; U.S. commander warns Beijing of challenges," *The Washington Times*, 28 May 2007.

[14] "Aircraft carrier competition looms over Asia-Pacific," *The Korean Herald*, 2 November 2007.

[15] Tim Fish, "China's first naval air cadets start training," *Jane's Navy International*, 11 Sep 2008.

[16] Andrew Jacobs, "General hints China's Navy wants to add carrier to fleet," *The New York Times*, 18 November 2008.

[17] "Chinese Military Denies Canadian Media Report which says that China has Started Building Aircraft Carrier in Shanghai," *Zhongguo Tongxun She* 中国通讯社 (Hong Kong), 28 November 2008.

[18] Richard Scott, "Chinese aircraft carrier capability unlikely before 2015, says U.S. report," *Jane's Navy International*, 31 Mar 2009.

[19] John Garnaut, "China drops hints about deploying an aircraft carrier," *Sydney Morning Herald*, 24 December 2008.

[20] Minnie Chan, "Carrier could trigger arms race," *South China Morning Post*, 12 January 2009.

[21] Richard Scott, "Chinese aircraft carrier capability unlikely before 2015, says U.S. report," *Jane's Navy International*. 31 Mar 2009.

[22] Hu Chen, "Justifiable and reasonable for China to have its own aircraft carriers," *Renmin Ribao* 人民日报 (China), 23 April 2009.

[23] Avinash Godbole and Sarabjeet Singh Parmar, *China's Aircraft Carrier: Some Observations*, Institute for Defence Studies and Analyses, 21 April 2011, http://www.idsa.in/idsacomments/ChinasAircraftCarrierSomeObservations_agodbole_210411.

[24] "Chinese Businessman bids £5m for UK's HMS Invincible," *BBC News*, 7 January 2011, http://www.bbc.co.uk/news/uk-12134071.

[25] Shuyan Wan, "China's First Aircraft Carrier is Not Intended for Combat Missions," *Zhongguo Xinwen She* 中国新文社 (China), 27 July 2011.

[26] Shan He, "China aircraft carrier begins 10th sea trial," *China Internet Information Center*, 28 August 2012, last accessed 21 May 2013, http://www.china.org.cn/china/2012-08/28/content_26353139.htm.

Drawing data points from the two earlier tables, Table 7 on the following page shows a side by side comparison of the *Varyag*'s actual developments and China's stated positions about carriers. It is clear that China started off with its official, overt interest in the *Varyag* from 1992 with a fairly consistent position that was coherent with actual developments. However, perhaps as a result of the experience of its failed 1992 purchase where U.S. and Japanese pressure on Ukraine is assessed to have scuttled the transfer, China adopted a more devious route towards it carrier acquisition.[142] When the Macau

---

[142] "Secret Chinese report on purchase of Ukrainian aircraft carrier," *Kyodo News Service*, 14 August 1992.

company acquired the *Varyag* in 1998, China treated it as a private commercial matter, minimizing its role in the process despite obvious state interest just six years earlier. However, the impasse over passage through the Bosphorus Straits compelled the state to negotiate with Turkey which was ultimately successful.[143]   Even then, China's state machinery minimized publicity on its role in the negotiations.   During the *Varyag*'s passage and even after its arrival in Dalian, China, China's state media minimized reporting on the *Varyag*, keeping its role ambiguous.   When refurbishment work started in earnest on *Varyag*, China never admitted to carrier construction or work on the *Varyag* specifically.   The closest it came to doing so was a 2007 statement that China would have carriers by 2010 which was then swiftly denied.   Only in 2011 did China admit to working specifically on a carrier.   At the same time however, China never hid its interest in carrier developments in general or its belief in the operational need for carriers.   This dichotomy between China's conceptual acceptance of carriers and its actual construction of such a capability is of interest to us in the study of China's employment of deception in the *Liaoning*'s development.

Table 7.   Comparison of *Varyag/Liaoning* Developments versus China's Positions about Carrier Development

Year	*Varyag/Liaoning* Development	China's Official Position	Consistent
1992	*Varyag* is put up for military sale.	China shows interest with military study delegation but deal falls through as result of U.S. and Japanese pressure on Ukraine.[144]	Yes
1998	*Varyag* is put up for scrap sale.	No official interest. Private company purchase.	Yes
2001	*Varyag* is stranded outside the Bosphorus Strait.	China acts on behalf of private company.	Yes
2002	*Varyag* berths at Dalian naval port.	China makes no statement. Maintains distance.	-
2003-2004	Superficial work begins on the *Varyag* but inconclusive as to carrier's functions.	China makes no statement. Maintains distance.	-
Continued on next page.			

---

143 "Turkey minister to convey message on carrier passage during China visit," *Anatolia News Agency*, 24 August 2001.

144 Secret Chinese report on purchase of Ukrainian aircraft carrier," *Kyodo News Service Tokyo*, 14 August 1992.

Continued from previous page.			
2005	*Varyag* painted in naval colors.	China denies carrier construction.	No
2006	U.S. and Taiwan assess the *Varyag* to be refurbished for naval training purposes.	China denies construction. PLA says carriers are useful and being studied.	No Yes
2007	U.S. D.O.D reports refurbishment of the *Varyag* for naval use but is unable to provide a clear estimate of completion.	PLA initially says carriers will be ready by 2010. PLA then denies any carrier construction. Commander of U.S. Pacific Fleet confirms China's interest in aircraft carrier capability.	Yes No Yes
2008	PLAN aviators begin carrier flight training.[145] *Varyag* refurbishment continues.	PLA says carrier capability is a national dream. PLA denies carrier construction. China reports that carrier confers status as major naval power commensurate with its rank.	Yes No Yes
2009	*Varyag* moved to larger dry dock for large scale engineering work.	China justifies conceptual need for carriers but admits no carrier construction.	Yes
2011	*Varyag* sea trials commence after weapon systems mounted.	China acknowledges carrier under construction for first time.	Yes.
2012	Commissioning of *Liaoning* into PLAN	China says carrier for research and training.	Yes

D.   RATIONALE FOR DECEPTION IN THE ACQUISITION OF CHINA'S AIRCRAFT CARRIER

From the examination of China's national and maritime goals in the earlier chapters, it was established that the acquisition of a carrier capability was consistent with China's long-term strategic goals.   Having established cause, the question of what motivated China's deception ploy regarding the *Varyag* remains.   As can be seen from the previous section, there was consideration disparity between China's public position of denial regarding the *Varyag*'s refurbishment and the reality of actual developments

---

[145] Fish, "China's first naval air cadets start training," *Jane's Navy International*.

onboard the *Varyag* in Dalian. This sections identifies the possible reasons for China to employ deception in its acquisition and development of its first aircraft carrier.

1. Rationale One: Disguise the Military Employment of its First Aircraft Carrier Acquisition

We posit that the first goal of Chinese deception on the acquisition of a carrier capability was to deflect any notion that it was seeking to acquire one for military purposes. Despite China's heavy marine industrial capability, China had no experience building a carrier and little knowledge about how to go about doing so, thus obtaining one that was already largely built would have been the prudent and most expedient option. However, given Chinese efforts to acquire an aircraft carrier in the 1990s, first from the Russians (*Varyag* in 1992), then the French (*Clemenceau* in 1995) and Brazilians (*SAC 200/220* in 1995); it would have been difficult for the Chinese to mask their goal of acquiring a carrier for military purposes.[146] To build a viable deception, the Chinese needed to build a different narrative about their interest in carriers and explore other means of acquiring the ships.

Fortuitously, the Chinese came across another way to acquire a carrier outside of the formal defence industry and country-to-country channels. Despite their unsuccessful attempts to acquire a carrier through official channels in the 1990s, the Chinese acquired the Australian Navy's retired flagship and carrier—the HMAS *Melbourne* in 1985. The *Melbourne* had been decommissioned in 1982 and the Australian government had approved its sale to a Chinese ship breaker for A$1.4 million in 1985 after its initial A$1.7 million sale to an Australian company in 1984 fell through.[147] As the *Melbourne* was broken up in Dalian, Chinese naval architects and engineers studied its design and construction.[148] The *Melbourne's* flight deck was preserved for Chinese pilots to practice carrier take-offs and landings ashore.[149] Despite Colonel General Xu Xing's

---

[146] Storey and You, "China's Aircraft Carrier Ambitions: Seeking Truth from Rumors," 78.

[147] "HMAS Melbourne (II)," *Royal Australian Navy*, last accessed 2 June 2013, http://www.navy.gov.au/hmas-melbourne-ii.

[148] Storey and You, "China's Aircraft Carrier Ambitions: Seeking Truth from Rumors," 78.

[149] Storey and You, "China's Aircraft Carrier Ambitions: Seeking Truth from Rumors," 78.

denial in 1987 that China wanted to acquire an aircraft carrier capability, China's interest in carriers in the 1990s proved otherwise.[150] Thus, with the *Melbourne* experience, the Chinese had now come upon a viable alternate means of acquiring aircraft carriers—albeit retired or scrap quality hulls without operational capabilities. The scrap acquisition method had been validated and had demonstrated utility for a modest capital outlay.

## 2.	Rationale Two: Outflank Opposition to China's Aircraft Carrier Ambitions

China expected opposition to its intention to acquire an aircraft carrier to enhance its military capability. Regional opposition from rival Japan and international opposition from its strategic competitor the United States were expected to be significant. In fact, the failed 1992 deal for China to purchase the *Varyag* from Ukraine through official government channels was presumably scuttled by U.S and Japanese pressure on Ukraine not to transfer carrier technology to China. Thus, China sought a way to acquire an aircraft carrier without arousing the opposition of known objectors. A deception ploy was therefore necessary to out-maneuver any official opposition to China's acquisition of an aircraft carrier—that meant that the Chinese state machinery could not be involved in the acquisition. Thus, the 1998 acquisition of the *Varyag* was spearheaded by a Macau-based private company and the Chinese state consciously distanced itself from any involvement.

## 3.	Rationale Three: Establish Organic Aircraft Carrier Construction Capability

From the beginning, China sought to purchase an existing hull rather than to build one from the keel up. Although buying rather than building one seemed detrimental to China's military industrial complex. From the perspective of establishing a national aircraft carrier building capability, there were two reasons that explain why this course may be beneficial in the long run. The first was the maturity and competency of China's warship building industry. As the world's leading commercial ship builder with 40% of global shipbuilding capacity, China certainly did not lack facilities or scale in its

---

[150] *Jian Chuan Zhi Shi* 舰船知识 (China), No.5, 1987, p.19.

shipbuilding industry.[151] However, building warships was a more complex task requiring higher levels of expertise across different skill areas. China's industry has mainly been focused on large volume construction of simpler commercial designs like bulk cargo carriers and small tankers despite state efforts to increase production of more complex vessels like cruise ships, very large crude oil carriers and gas carriers.[152] By buying a carrier and refurbishing it, China allowed its industry to take progressive steps in building its capabilities and fine-tuning itself for the eventual task of building a carrier from scratch. The additional time also allowed for commercial modernization to take effect as China's shipbuilding industry continued to make qualitative improvements.

The second reason for acquiring a carrier rather than building one is that China may be seeking a conservative, progressive approach towards building its carrier capability. For comparison, each modern aircraft carrier in the U.S. CVN-21 carrier program is estimated to cost around US$12 billion. [153] Rather than embarking on the expensive construction of a new aircraft carrier with the attendant risks of building one from the keel up for the first time, China sought a more pragmatic approach. Acquiring a partially built or used aircraft carrier would not only have been more economical, in the long term it would also prove more beneficial to the strength of China's nascent aircraft carrier program. By first operating an aircraft carrier, China can better understand her operational requirements and eventually build one according to the lessons learnedfrom operating her first carrier. This would be critical in determining the capabilities that China would need in the shipbuilding, aviation, electronics and other associated industries so that she may build a capable carrier appropriate to her needs.

Lastly, in terms of fielding an aircraft carrier for immediate operational use, acquiring a partially constructed one would certainly have shortened the lead-time

---

151 "2012 World Shipping Statistics," *IHS,* last accessed 4 June 2013, http://www.ihs.com/products/maritime-information/statistics-forecasts/world-shipbuilding.aspx.

152 Gabriel Collins and Michael C. Grubb, *A Comprehensive Survey of China's Dynamic Shipbuilding Industry*, U.S. Naval War College: China Maritime Studies, (Newport, Rhode Island: Naval War College Press, 2008), 3.

153 Ronald O'Rourke, *Navy CVN-21 Aircraft Carrier Program: Background and Issues for Congress*, CRS Report RS20643 (Washington, DC: Library of Congress, Congressional Research Service, 25 May 2005).

compared to building such a complex warship for the first time. Fielding an aircraft carrier earlier would also allow for associated developments in carrier aviation and doctrine development to be accelerated. Therefore, for China there were compelling reasons to buy rather than build her first aircraft carrier.

The rationale for China to employ strategic deception in the acquisition of her first aircraft carrier is compelling and very much driven by her 1992 experience in failing to acquire the *Varyag* the first time around. The next section proposes how China could have employed strategic deception in the acquisition of its first aircraft carrier.

E. THE TRIPLE LAYERED SOVIET COVER: *MINSK, VARYAG* AND *KIEV*

China's experience with the HMAS *Melbourne* revealed an alternate path to acquire the body of an aircraft carrier through scrap acquisition. Accordingly, the first step in the formulation of its strategic deception was to develop a believable cover story. The Chinese proved resourceful, creative and enterprising in building a narrative around the aircraft carrier amusement park. Between 1995 and 2000, private Chinese companies acquired three ex-Soviet carriers—the *Minsk, Varyag* and *Kiev* as hulls intended for scrap. All three were eventually kept intact after their transfer to China in an intriguing chain of events.

The flagship of the Soviet Pacific Fleet, *Minsk*, was decommissioned from the Russian Navy in 1993 and sold in 1995 to a South Korean company for scrap. In June 1998, a Chinese firm, the *Minsk* Aircraft Carrier Industry, bought the *Minsk* for five million dollars under the condition that it would not be used for military purposes.[154] The *Minsk* was subsequently towed to Guangdong for a four million dollar conversion into a floating museum and finally relocated to Shenzhen where it became the centerpiece of the "*Minsk* World" military theme park.[155]

In March 1998, the *Varyag* was acquired by the Macau-based private company Chong Lot for 20 million dollars—three times its scrap value. In November 1998, Chong

---

[154] "Mainland Firm Buys Aircraft Carrier," *South China Morning Post*, 3 September 1998.

[155] "*Minsk* World", last accessed 2 June 2013, http://www.sz*Minsk*.com/park/.

Lot declared that the *Varyag* would be turned into a floating casino and entertainment complex anchored in Macau harbour.[156] Was it pure coincidence that both the *Minsk* and *Varyag* plans for conversion into entertainment platforms would dovetail nicely in the second half of 1998? Does the fact that the *Varyag* charted such a different course from the *Minsk* at the end not evoke suspicion—with the *Varyag* being re-commissioned into the PLAN as a sea-worthy aircraft carrier? If the purchase of the *Minsk* and *Varyag* were indeed part of an elaborate Chinese deception, what role did the acquisition of the *Kiev* play then?

In May 2000, the *Kiev* was purchased from the Russian government by the Tianma Shipbreaking Company based in Tianjin, China for $8.4 million.[157] In November 2000, the original contract that stipulated the scrapping of *Kiev* was re-negotiated between the Chinese and Russian governments to allow for the *Kiev* to be used for tourism purposes.[158] After a £9.6m refit, the *Kiev* was re-opened to the public in Feb 2012 as a tourist attraction and hotel.[159] What role did the *Kiev* play in China's deception cover story given that both the *Minsk* and *Varyag* had already laid the foundations of the deception narrative? The authors believe the *Kiev* served as a second red-herring to deflect attention from the *Varyag* and to give the amusement park narrative further credibility so that any lingering suspicion arising from the investigations of *Varyag*'s true purpose would be dispelled. At the time of the *Kiev* acquisition in 2000, the *Varyag* was still stuck in the Black Sea due to Turkey barring her passage through the Bosphorus Strait. Publicity over the *Varyag*'s difficulties would have been unwelcome to the Chinese deception ploy.

The authors propose that the timing of the acquisition of the *Minsk*, *Varyag* and *Kiev;* and the cover story concerning their conversion into entertainment centers were an elaborate deception by the Chinese to achieve their goal of acquiring a carrier that would

---

[156] "$1.6b Hotel Plan for Warship," *South China Morning Post*, 11 November 1998.

[157] "Kiev Sale to China Will Not Tilt Power Balance," *Straits Times*, 10 May 2000.

[158] Storey and You, "China's Aircraft Carrier Ambitions: Seeking Truth from Rumors," 83.

[159] "China launches second aircraft carrier after a £9.6m refit…as a luxury hotel," *Daily Mail (UK)*, 10 August 2011, http://www.dailymail.co.uk/news/article-2024729/China-launches-second-aircraft-carrier-9-6m-refit--luxury-hotel.html?ITO=1490.

eventually be made sea-worthy again. First, we know that China's interest in the *Varyag* existed based on their inquiries with the Ukrainian government and the failed transfer in 1992. Second, the short window between 1998 to 2000 was used to make the acquisition of the three carriers *Minsk*, *Varyag* and *Kiev* to minimize exposure, confuse scrutiny and intensify the deception. Third, the *Varyag* was likely identified to be the platform for resuscitation early on and the *Minsk* and *Kiev* were acquired not only for technical investigations but also as red-herrings to divert any investigation into the *Varyag* and strengthen the cover story.

Fourth, the order of acquisition and development of the three carriers supports the narrative and desired outcome of the deception. Although the *Varyag* was acquired first, the *Minsk* was developed into an entertainment center much earlier (by 2004). This essentially allowed the *Minsk* to set the tone for the cover story and be the primary vehicle for its development. The *Varyag,* due to its location in the Black Sea, would take almost 4 years to complete its transit to China in Mar 2002. This is where the *Kiev* came into the narrative to sustain the cover story about China's interest in aircraft carrier themed entertainment centers and to deflect attention away from the tortuous transfer of the *Varyag*. Due to the difficulties associated with the acquisition and transfer of the *Varyag*, the *Kiev* served as timely foil to sustain the cover story and buy time for the transfer of the *Varyag* to be completed.

F.   DECEPTION MANAGEMENT BY CHINA

Assuming that the Chinese had attempted to deceive the world about the development of the *Varyag*, it would still have been necessary to manage the deception plot to sustain the deception. Whenever reports surfaced about China's development of the *Varyag* or a carrier capability, the Chinese found it necessary to contradict, confuse or otherwise deny information so that no correct, definitive conclusion could be made. This section studies the various means used by the Chinese to manage their deception regarding the development of the *Varyag* specifically and China's aircraft carrier capabilities in general. There were three broad approaches that the Chinese used to manage the deception about the *Varyag*. First, China maintained the *Varyag*'s cover story for as long as it could. Second, China never denied interest in the value of an aircraft carrier capability. Third, China employed contradictory messaging to confuse the truth with deceit.

1.   Maintenance of Cover Narrative about the *Varyag*'s Purpose

The PLA maintained a single cover narrative to explain the purpose of the *Varyag* purchase—conversion into a floating casino. Regardless of the difficulties the Chinese encountered in transporting the *Varyag* to China and foreign intelligence estimates, China never wavered in its narrative on the *Varyag*'s purpose. This was important for a few reasons:

Minimize suspicion and scrutiny. China maintained the cover story through the *Varyag*'s arrival in China in 2002 and after that until official acknowledgement that the *Varyag* was being refurbished as a carrier in 2011. From the point of purchase in 1998 to 2011, the Chinese had to sustain the cover story for 13 years and try to hide the true function of something as large and recognizable as an aircraft carrier. Although foreign interests postulated the development of an aircraft carrier capability by China throughout the period, the *Varyag* was not always the focus of attention. There were numerous assessments that were made in those 13 years that made no reference to the *Varyag* and instead postulated about the construction of new build carriers. The earliest accurate assessments of the actual role of the *Varyag* were made in 2005 by *Jane's* and in 2006 by U.S. and Taiwanese analysts who correctly surmised that the *Varyag* was being refurbished as an aircraft carrier training platform.[160] China denied those claims. China adroitly avoided making references to the *Varyag* whenever possible and merely issued denials to any claims about the *Varyag* without volunteering additional information. This strategy of sticking to staid uninformative denials allowed China to wear down the resistance and curiosity of foreign intelligence. Even though the *Varyag* was berthed in plain view to the Chinese public, the interminable stance taken by the Chinese kept interest levels in the *Varyag* to a minimum and probably led to *Varyag*-fatigue in reporting agencies—which would have served Chinese interests.

---

[160] Lague, "Do China's strategic ambitions include a carrier?"

Allow other elements of the deception ploy (*Kiev* and *Minsk*) to serve supporting roles. By maintaining its cover story of carrier-themed entertainment, China would constantly point to the *Kiev* and *Minsk* as evidence that its acquisition of old carriers was for scientific and economic purposes and not military ends. It is also telling to note that whenever China made references to the *Kiev* and *Minsk*, it would not make any reference to the *Varyag*, like it last did in 2007.[161] This was a deliberate attempt to allow the <u>*Varyag*</u> to fall out of the limelight. However, to knowing external observers, this glaring omission should have aroused suspicion and further reinforce the argument that China's intention was to hide the true purpose of the *Varyag*. Fortunately for China, curiosity about the *Varyag* never reached troublesome levels and the development of the *Varyag* was never jeopardized.

<u>Maximize probability of success for the transfer of the *Varyag*</u>. The most critical phase of the *Varyag*'s development was its successful transfer to China. If foreign powers had learned of the *Varyag*'s true purpose, various diplomatic and military measures could have been imposed to disrupt her transit or even sabotage the rusting hulk itself. Once the *Varyag* was in Chinese waters, the most vulnerable phase of the *Varyag*'s development would have been successfully overcome. There were actually two occasions during the *Varyag*'s voyage that it encountered foreign interventions. The first was Turkey's opposition to its transit of the Bosphorus Strait that caught China by surprise and led to the significant 15 month confinement of the *Varyag* in the Black Sea. The second incident happened while the *Varyag* was doing tug-towed circuits within the Black Sea when an unidentified helicopter landed on the *Varyag* and disembarked three men who appeared to take measurements of the ship. They left before the *Varyag*'s tug crew arrived onboard and reportedly scrawled "The French was here" on the *Varyag*'s deck.[162] The first incident was resolved through diplomacy, the second was quietly forgotten. While neither incident ultimately stopped China's plans to develop the

---

161 Chuang, "Chinese Navy Expert refutes 'Aircraft Carrier Threat' Theory'".

162 John Ward Anderson, "Turks Keep Ship Going Round in Circles; It's no Longer A Carrier, Not Yet a Casino," *The Washington Post*, 22 July 2001, A18.

Varyag, the incidents portended what could have been more serious attempts to sink China's carrier ambitions for the *Varyag*.

Minimize expectations about Chinese technical ability. There was also the under-estimation by the West of *Varyag*'s viability as a possible hull for eventual reconstitution as an operational aircraft carrier as well as China's technical capability to complete such a task.[163] China never publicly contradicted Western perceptions about its perceived weaknesses which would have undermined China's interests in reducing attention and obstruction to its construction of the *Varyag*. Chinese strategic philosophy encourages such a posture through the concepts of "hide and bide" espoused within Deng Xiaopoing's "24 Character Strategy" and "feigning foolishness even if not insane" from the Thirty-Six Stratagems.[164] The most significant sign of the success of this strategy was the assertion from the Asia-Pacific editor of *Jane's Defense Weekly* that the *Varyag* "has been sitting around too long in too unclean conditions to be used as an operational warship," and that "China is a sovereign country. It's unlikely they would go through the charade of using a front company in Macau. They don't have to sneak around."[165] How wrong *Jane's* was on both counts, much to the relief of China.

2. Never Denying Chinese Interest in Aircraft Carrier Capability

China never denied its interest in aircraft carriers and acknowledged the strengths that a carrier could add to the PLA's military capabilities. China knew that its institutional interest in aircraft carriers was well known through the PLAN commander and Central Military Commission Vice-Chairman Liu Huaqing's assertions in the 1980s and never sought to conceal such an interest.[166] At the same time, China downplayed security concerns that might arise from any future carrier capability by emphasizing the

---

[163] Scott, "Chinese aircraft carrier capability unlikely before 2015, says U.S. report."

[164] Refer to Chapter V on Deception.

[165] Anderson, "Turks Keep Ship Going Round in Circles; It's no Longer A Carrier, Not Yet a Casino."

[166] Storey and You, "China's Aircraft Carrier Ambitions: Seeking Truth from Rumors."

territorial security (as opposed to regional power projection) and non-combat roles of the carrier in providing humanitarian and disaster assistance.[167]

This was a sensible long-term strategy for China as it would have been disingenuous of the Chinese if they denied ever having an interest in aircraft carriers, only to operationalize one later in the future. Thus China never sought to deny its interest in possessing such a capability. Instead, it held close to its chest the building and realization of such a capability. This strategy reduced unwanted attention on its carrier development programs because if China had denied any interest in carrier capabilities, it may have triggered investigative attempts to prove otherwise. However, by admitting interest, China could overtly carry on its research and development programs for a carrier capability without undue attention or suspicion. China's positive position regarding carriers also facilitated its carrier-associated acquisitions of technology or material from its partners without undue alarm. This strategy allowed the construction of the *Varyag* to proceed without an internal contradiction within the Chinese system and without having to deal with any controversy that may have been stirred by outright denial about any interest in carrier capability.

Maintaining a positive position on aircraft carrier capability also allowed the Chinese to better maintain their overall deception by pulling other elements into play that would not have been available if they had issued an outright denial of interest. These including self-deception by foreign intelligence about new aircraft carrier constructions in China and the actual completion of *Varyag*'s refurbishment (which were mostly too pessimistic). In essence, open interest in an aircraft carrier capability not only served the strategic needs of concealing *Varyag*'s refurbishment, it also served China's broader strategic military calculus and allowed considerable uncertainty to be injected into the strategic considerations of competing states.

China's declared interest in developing an aircraft carrier capability was the wiser strategic choice compared to outright denial. A denial would have imposed an inordinate amount of constraint on its research and development efforts as well as a publicity

---

[167] Shuyan Wan, "China's First Aircraft Carrier is Not Intended for Combat Missions."

nightmare with the *Varyag* largely in plain sight in the Dalian shipyard. Thus, China's openness about its interest in carriers was a master stroke in perception management and protecting its deception regarding the *Varyag*.

3. Employing Contradictory Signals to Confuse

While China never hid its aspiration for a carrier capability, it was never clear about when it would build one to fulfill that aspiration. Chinese and foreign reports about carriers being built only served to confuse and perhaps conceal the development of the *Varyag* under the suspicion of other spurious programs. China came out several times to deny carrier construction projects—one in April 2007 even citing the *Minsk* and *Kiev* as examples to the contrary.[168] Between 2002 (when *Varyag* arrived in China) and 2011 (when the *Varyag*'s refurbishment was officially acknowledged), the PLA consistently denied construction of aircraft carriers in 2005, 2006, 2007, 2008. *Jane's* 2005 revelation that the *Varyag* had been repainted in PLAN colors represented a watershed in foreign assessment of *Varyag*'s true purpose because it was the clearest indicator of the role intended for *Varyag*. *Jane's* had discredited the casino cover story.[169] Even so, China stuck to its cover story about a non-military role for *Varyag* (as evidenced by its 2007 assertion) and never publicly acknowledged the actual role of the *Varyag* until the official announcement in 2011. This Chinese poker-face when *Jane's* had effectively called its bluff in 2005 was essential to maintaining its deception and denying foreign intelligence what would have been confirmation of *Varyag*'s role more than 7 years before it was commissioned.

While Chinese denials of carrier construction were perhaps expected, China also unexpectedly moved in the opposite direction on the question of developing aircraft carrier capabilities. The most telling example is the Commander of the U.S. Pacific Fleet's comment that all the Chinese leaders he met on a visit in May 2007 had voiced considerable interest about developing aircraft carriers.[170] What is the reason for this

---

[168] Kung-pai Chuang, "Chinese Navy Expert refutes 'Aircraft Carrier Threat' Theory."

[169] "Is China building a carrier?" *Jane's Defence Weekly.*

[170] Halloran and Gertz, "China intent on aircraft carrier goal; U.S. commander warns Beijing of challenges."

apparently contradictory behavior by China within the space of two months in 2007—with a denial about construction issued in April and interest in carrier construction stated by Chinese leaders meeting the most senior military leader in charge of the Pacific region in May?[171] Was it poor coordination by the Chinese to maintain their policy lines regarding carriers? Or was it a deliberate attempt to send mixed signals and confuse foreign intelligence? The authors believe it latter reason may be valid because each message was targeted at a specific audience to achieve specific goals.

The first message involving denial of carrier construction was broadcast on Chinese television and ostensibly targeted the Chinese domestic audience to debunk the "Chinese carrier threat theory" espoused by foreign governments and to educate them about the justifications for Chinese self-determination in terms of military capability development. The second message was not directed at a broad audience but at an individual leader of a competing military system who would influence security policy in Asia. The Chinese would not have known whether comments made to the U.S. Commander of Pacific Command, Admiral Timothy J. Keating, would have been transmitted to the public realm but they certainly left him in no doubt about their interest in developing an aircraft carrier capability.[172] That Admiral Keating was only two months into his Pacific command tour when he visited China may have urged the Chinese to cultivate an impression in him about their carrier ambitions for reasons of strategic posture.

Whatever the reasons may have been, the near simultaneous denial of carrier construction and declaration of interest in carriers would have been confusing to foreign observers and the Chinese may have wanted nothing more than to inject doubt and uncertainty into foreign projections regarding China's carrier capability. To leave the adversary guessing may not be the ideal end state in typical deception ploys because the deceiver would normally want the deceived to fall into a specific position of belief.

---

[171] Kung-pai Chuang, "Chinese Navy Expert refutes 'Aircraft Carrier Threat' Theory." Senior Captain Li Jie, a research fellow at the Military Academic Research Institute of the Chinese Navy, refuted foreign assertions about China's carrier threat and referenced the *Minsk* and *Kiev* as evidence to refute foreign claims.

[172] "Admiral Timothy J. Keating," *United States Navy Biography*, last updated 3 December 2008, http://www.navy.mil/navydata/bios/navybio.asp?bioID=22

However, in the case of China's aircraft carrier development, to leave foreign intelligence in a state of uncertainty about the true intent for *Varyag* may have been a favorable end state given the significant physical evidence of the *Varyag* being refurbished in plain sight of the world.

The arguments above have shown that through material (*Kiev* and *Minsk*) and psychological measures, China was able to manage its deception about the *Varyag*'s intended refurbishment into a functional aircraft carrier and establish an important foothold in the long term development of a viable aircraft carrier capability for the PLAN. While the deception surrounding the *Varyag* neither masked its existence nor hid the fact that China was interested in developing a carrier capability; the deception ploy was sufficiently effective to allow China to develop the *Varyag* to operational status through the achievement of the following objectives:

- Acquire the *Varyag* in the face of reluctance from Ukraine; competing acquisition attempts from competitors; and regional and global concerns about Chinese military modernization.

- Physically relocate the *Varyag* from the Black Sea to China's coast through a tortuous voyage that not only caused delays but potentially threatened the transfer of the *Varyag* back to China. The economic cost and physical difficulty of the *Varyag*'s voyage were real threats to the viability of the Chinese plans for the *Varyag*.

- Refurbish and rebuild the *Varyag* in China over a period of more than 10 years under international and regional scrutiny without significant obstacles and negative publicity. During this time, there were many postulations about China's potential carrier capability and estimations about when such a capability would be achieved. Few proved to be right and even the correct suspicions were sufficiently covered by the overall Chinese deception that they never amounted to much.

- Achieve a public relations coup when the *Varyag* was officially commissioned into the PLAN. The *Varyag* symbolized not just the triumph of Chinese military planning and industrial expertise, but also carried the hopes of a nation and had a symbolic significance that far outweighed its military utility. It also represented Chinese triumph in the face of regional and international obstacles; and most significantly, it became a symbol of defiance to the hegemony of the United States in East Asia which was most evidently embodied in its aircraft carrier battle groups in the Pacific.

G. CONCLUSION

This chapter has examined the strategic deception employed by China to ensure that is plans for the acquisition and development of the former Russian carrier *Varyag* into its first aircraft carrier the *Liaoning* achieved fruition. By contrasting China's official position on aircraft carriers and its intentions for the *Liaoning* with the reality of the refurbishment work that was done on the *Liaoning*, the duplicity of China's deception was pointed out. The motivation behind China's deception and the mechanics of the *Liaoning* deception were elaborated to provide deeper understanding of the deception ploy's genesis and evolution. Finally, the measures taken by China to maximize the effects of the *Liaoning* deception were elaborated to explain China's actions and statements as the *Liaoning* deception played out to its logical conclusion.

The *Liaoning* deception the world has witnessed may have only been the first phase of a larger plan to mask China's development of a larger carrier force and capability. Now that the deception surrounding the *Liaoning*'s acquisition and development has been explained, the next chapter investigates the possible roles that could be undertaken by the *Liaoning* as China's first aircraft carrier. The findings about *Liaoning*'s role will provide some indication of the trajectory to be expected as China develops its carrier capability and hopefully provide observers with greater insight to penetrate the fog of China's deception.

THIS PAGE INTENTIONALLY LEFT BLANK

VII. ANALYSIS OF COMPETING HYPOTHESES FOR THE ROLE OF CHINA'S FIRST AIRCRAFT CARRIER

A. INTRODUCTION

Chapter V examined strategic deception with Chinese characteristics while Chapter VI investigated the intricacies of the *Liaoning* deception. This chapter shall employ Richards Heuer's Analysis of Competitive Hypotheses (ACH) to assess the likely roles to be performed by China's first aircraft carrier *Liaoning* as it matures into service with the PLAN.

The purpose of this analysis is to determine the most likely role for the *Liaoning*. The rationale for this analysis is driven by China's assertion that the *Liaoning* is to be used for "research and training purposes." While the carrier will undoubtedly be employed for such purposes as China continues to build and strengthen its carrier capability, the question is whether the *Liaoning* will play a bigger role than mere research and training. Thus, this chapter will employ Heuer's ACH to assess if China is revealing only a small portion of the *Liaoning*'s actual role in China's maritime strategy. The findings from ACH should reveal if China is being economical with the truth and employing deception to mask the *Liaoning*'s true roles in the PLAN.

B. THE ROLE OF CHINA'S FIRST AIRCRAFT CARRIER—THE *LIAONING*

On 27 July 2011, China revealed to the world that her first aircraft carrier —the *Liaoning* was under construction. In the same report, Rear Admiral Zhang Zhaozhong, a professor at the PLA's National Defense University pointed out that "China's first aircraft carrier will not perform combat missions. Instead, it will be mainly used for training and experimentation purposes."[173] He elaborated that training activities would include "training personnel working on carrier platforms, pilots of carrier-based aircraft and operators of the carrier.[174]" He also explained that experimentation would include

---

[173] Wan, "China's First Aircraft Carrier is Not Intended for Combat Missions."

[174] Wan, "China's First Aircraft Carrier is Not Intended for Combat Missions."

ironing out compatibility issues between the various systems onboard; evaluation of the carrier and its equipment and systems; and examination of carrier design and building technologies.[175] During the commissioning of the *Liaoning*, China reaffirmed *Liaoning*'s training and research roles. The 2012 U.S. DOD report to Congress on China's military developments echoed similar expectations for the *Liaoning*'s role.[176]

Why does an accurate understanding of the *Liaoning*'s role matter? It is critical to understanding China's broader strategy concerning aircraft carriers and estimating the possible role that the *Liaoning* may play in the unforeseen scenarios that may arise in the near future. A clear understanding of the *Liaoning*'s potential and its role will allow for better assessment of the strategic situation and allow interested countries to adopt the necessary measures to deal with the *Liaoning*'s envisaged role.

C.   THEORY OF ANALYSIS OF COMPETITIVE HYPOTHESES

Heuer conceptualized ACH as "a tool to aid judgement on important issues requiring careful weighting of alternative explanations or conclusions."[177] ACH has been influential in refining intelligence analysis and has been used by intelligence agencies to improve their analysis of information and make more refined assessments.[178] At the core of ACH is the notion of competition among plausible hypotheses to determine which ones survive a gauntlet of testing with available information.[179] Heuer outlined eight steps for the execution of ACH and the following sections will discuss all eight as we try to determine the most probable role for the *Liaoning* as China's first aircraft carrier.

---

[175] Wan, "China's First Aircraft Carrier is Not Intended for Combat Missions."

[176] Office of the Secretary of Defense, *Annual Report to Congress: Military and Security Developments Involving the People's Republic of China 2012*, May 2012, http://www.defense.gov/pubs/pdfs/2012_cmpr_final.pdf.

[177] Heuer, *Psychology of Intelligence Analysis,* 95.

[178] Heuer, *Psychology of Intelligence Analysis,* xxiii.

[179] Heuer, *Psychology of Intelligence Analysis,* 95.

Step 1: Identifying Competing Hypotheses

The first step in ACH calls for the identification of all possible hypotheses pertaining to the issue of interest—the role of the *Liaoning* as China's first aircraft carrier.

Hypothesis 1 (H1): The *Liaoning* will spearhead the operational deployment of China's aircraft carrier capability.

Our first hypothesis (H1) postulates that the *Liaoning* will spearhead the operational deployment of China's aircraft carriers. H1 basically refutes China's claims that the *Liaoning* will only be used for research and training purposes. H1 believes that the *Liaoning*'s role will extend beyond research and training and will eventually encompass operational capability in the full spectrum of operations for China's first aircraft carrier. H1 assesses that the *Liaoning* will be deployed for actual operations where necessary and will be a flagship for operations when it is deployed. H1 suggests that the *Liaoning* will naturally ascend to the position of flagship for the PLAN and be a warship of special significance and symbolic importance to China. H1 is the most optimistic assessment of the *Liaoning*'s capabilities and accords it a wide and expansive role.

Hypothesis 2 (H2): The *Liaoning* will serve only a limited research and training role.

The second hypothesis (H2) suggests that the *Liaoning* will only perform research and training duties within the PLAN. H2 takes China's proclamation about the *Liaoning*'s role at face value and postulates that the *Liaoning*'s development will not reach full operational capability as a warship. H2 would see the *Liaoning* gradually fade into obscurity as the PLAN's aircraft carrier capability improves and new carriers replace the *Liaoning* as the symbolic figurehead of the PLAN. H2 represents a conservative estimate of the *Liaoning*'s capabilities and accords it a limited role.

Hypothesis 3 (H3): The *Liaoning* will be an operational failure, unable to fulfill even its designated role in research and training.

The third hypothesis (H3) suggests that the *Liaoning* is incapable of performing its stated roles of research and training.   H3 suggests that either due to design inadequacies, technical limitations, environmental constraints or strategic considerations, the *Liaoning* will not be able to fulfill the roles that China has envisaged for her. She would become the PLAN's floating 60,000 ton white elephant that is not deployable for research, training or operations. H3 includes constraints on the *Liaoning*'s deployment from within the Chinese system like inadequate resource allocation for the carrier's operation (environmental constraint), and from the international environment like political pressure from regional countries or the U.S. (strategic considerations). H3 suggests the worst case scenario for the *Liaoning* and represents the most pessimistic hypothesis for *Liaoning*'s future role.

Disproved Hypothesis: The *Liaoning* as a commercial entertainment facility.

When formulating hypotheses, Heuer urges caution in differentiating between *unproven* ones and *disproved* ones.[180] In formulating possible hypotheses, we want to avoid the error of omitting unproven hypotheses as opposed to disproved ones. One of the disproved hypothesis in the consideration of the *Liaoning*'s role is its potential as a commercial entertainment facility. This was the role used as a cover for China's deception during the acquisition and development of the *Varyag* into the *Liaoning*. This hypothesis was clearly disproved by the commissioning of *Liaoning* into the PLAN on 25 September 2012 and the huge investments made in ensuring that the ship is seaworthy and suitable for carrier flight operations. Therefore it will not be considered among the possible hypotheses.

Step 2: Listing of Consistent and Inconsistent Evidence and Arguments for Hypotheses

The second step of ACH calls for the listing of evidence and arguments for each hypothesis. Heuer advises an expansive definition of evidence and for the inclusion of

---

[180] Heuer, *Psychology of Intelligence Analysis,* 98.

assumptions and logical deductions about the subject of study as these generate "strong preconceptions of which hypothesis is most likely.[181]

Hypothesis 1: Consistent and Inconsistent Evidence and Arguments

Evidence consistent with H1 that the *Liaoning* will spearhead operational deployment of China's aircraft carrier capability is as follows:

1. The *Liaoning* was touted as a "landmark in the country's modernization of armed forces and national defense" by the Chinese government.[182] If the *Liaoning* is indeed perceived by China to be a symbol of its military's modernization and ability, it would be counter-intuitive to limit its role to mere research and training.

2. Once operational capabilities are built up, the transition from research and training to actual operational deployment is easily achieved. In fact, most naval ships deployed for operations are in a constant state of internal training for their ship's crews, so the transition from training to operations hardly requires a stretch of the imagination.

3. The *Liaoning* is a capable warship in its own right. Although the *Liaoning* was built from the hull of a scrapped carrier, its internal machinery and systems are presumably modern having only been recently installed during refurbishment. Thus, as a naval platform, the *Liaoning* is no laggard based on outdated technology. In terms of size, the *Liaoning* is only 30 meters shorter (300m versus 330m) than the Nimitz-class carriers that are the most modern class of carriers in current service.[183] Although the *Liaoning* is significantly lighter (67,000 ton versus 100,000 ton displacement) than the Nimitz-class, it is by no means a small carrier. Thus the *Liaoning* is a capable warship by any standard.

4. The difficulty of producing aircraft carriers means that the *Liaoning* must hold the operational fort for some time yet. Although China's shipbuilding industry made impressive strides in recent decades, construction of a modern aircraft carrier is complex and demanding work. The previous chapter outlined the difficulties of carrier construction for China—which explained why China acquired the *Varyag* instead of constructing a carrier of its own. That being the case, it would be hard to fathom that the *Liaoning* would not be deployed for operations if it was capable and the need arose.

---

[181] Heuer, *Psychology of Intelligence Analysis*, 99.

[182] "No need to panic about China's aircraft carrier," *Xinhua* (China), 26 September 2012.

[183] Jonathan Marcus, "China extending military reach," *BBC News Asia-Pacific*, 14 June 2011, http://www.bbc.co.uk/news/world-asia-pacific-13761711.

5.   To restrict the *Liaoning* to research and training roles would be a great waste of resources. China invested at least US$26 million just to acquire and tow the *Varyag* back to China.[184] There is no estimate on the cost of refurbishing and equipping the *Varyag* to bring it up to operational condition. The operating cost of the carrier must also be significant. Taking these into account, it would appear that a limitation on the *Liaoning*'s role to mere training and research would be short-sighted. Moreover, modern carriers can operate for up to 50 years.[185] The *Liaoning*'s role must be expected to grow as it matures and it is only natural that as its capability grows, its operational utility would expand beyond training and research.

6.   The *Liaoning* has significant operational value as the largest warship and possibly most capable aircraft carrier of its size in the East Asia region. The PLAN is already the largest navy in the Asia Pacific region and although fleet size is not the best indicator of operational effectiveness, it is an indicator of operational reach and enduring naval presence that is of great value in the context of peacetime engagement and limited conflict.

7.   Operational urgency may compel China to deploy *Liaoning* for operations. Tensions in the East and South China Seas are rising after the 2009 submissions of territorial claims to the United Nations. Frequent naval confrontations between China and regional competitors have raised the stakes and may compel China to deploy the *Liaoning* to strengthen its ability to protect its territorial claims.

8.   Father of China's maritime strategy - Admiral Liu Huaqing's plan was to deploy the aircraft carrier to the South China Sea.[186] The late Liu Huaqing had stated in his memoirs that China would need to deploy aircraft carriers to the South China Sea to protect its sea lines of communications. The trajectory of China's naval development so far has been largely in concert with the maritime strategy laid out of Liu. It appears more likely than not that the *Liaoning* will be deployed for an operational role in the South China Sea once she is ready.

Evidence inconsistent with H1's assertion that the *Liaoning* will spearhead operational deployment of China's aircraft carrier capability is as follows:

1.   The *Liaoning* will not be ready for operational deployment. Aircraft carriers need aircraft and the *Liaoning* was commissioned without an organic fighter wing. Carrier aviation is still in its infancy in China and it will not be possible for China to stand up a full aircraft carrier capability

---

[184] "China pays S$45m for carrier hull," *The Straits Times* (Singapore), 6 March 2002.

[185] "Aircraft Carriers – CVN," *United States Navy Fact File*, updated 23 October 2012, http://www.navy.mil/navydata/fact_display.asp?cid=4200&tid=200&ct=4

[186] Paul, "The great Chinese aircraft carrier mystery."

94

within a short time window. In May 2013, China just stood up its first carrier aviation wing, but the number of trained pilots is still very small and it will take years to build up a sustainable pool of pilots.[187]

2. One aircraft carrier is insufficient for sustainable operational deployment[188]. Naval operations typically require at least three naval platforms of any type for sustainable operations. While one is in operation, the second one is being worked up for deployment and the third is undergoing maintenance. All naval ships go through a similar deployment cycle and having just one carrier makes it extremely taxing on the ship and its crew for sustained operations. Thus, it is unlikely that the *Liaoning* will be deployed for sustained operations.

3. Deploying the *Liaoning* for operations would be too aggressive and counter to China's assertions that it believes in peaceful development and the resolution of disputes without force. China has repeatedly asserted its belief in peaceful development and its belief in the peaceful resolution of issues.[189] Deploying the *Liaoning* for operations in the South China East would be viewed by regional countries as an escalation of force and would be contrary to China's diplomatic assertions.[190]

4. Rest of the PLAN may not be ready to support *Liaoning* with the protective carrier escort due to lack of suitable ships, doctrinal clarity and capabilities. Without a proper escort, an aircraft carrier becomes a high-value target for adversaries and China may be unwilling to risk its first and only carrier.

5. China wants the world to believe the *Liaoning* is only for research and training. This narrative would best serve China's interests as it downplays the potential military value of the *Liaoning* as well as obscuring the expected enhancements that will be made to the *Liaoning* as the ship, naval aviation, operating doctrines and procedures are enhanced over time.

Hypothesis 2: Consistent and Inconsistent Evidence and Arguments

Evidence consistent with H2's assertion that the *Liaoning* will only be used for research and training purposes is as follows:

1. The official position of China on the *Liaoning*'s role is its use for research and training purposes. While China has not said that the *Liaoning* will only be restricted to such a role, it has also emphasized the importance of research and training at this stage of China's carrier capability

---

[187] "China forms its first carrier aviation unit," *People's Daily Online* (China), 11 May 2013, http://english.peopledaily.com.cn/90786/8240574.html.

[188] "*Liaoning*'s role in China's Navy," *South China Morning Post*, 1 October 2012, 10.

[189] Wan, "China's First Aircraft Carrier is Not Intended for Combat Missions."

[190] "*Liaoning*'s role in China's Navy," *South China Morning Post*, 1 October 2012, 10.

development. China stands to gain much goodwill and build trust by sticking to its non-aggressive deployment plans for the *Liaoning*.

2. It is logical for research and training to be the *Liaoning*'s first priority because it is the first platform of a brand new capability for China. Therefore, there are many areas in which China has to conduct research and training to realize new capabilities. Carrier aviation is one significant area of research and training for the PLAN and it is apparent from recent developments that substantial training will still be required to generate the requisite quantity and quality of carrier pilots.

3. Research and training is more beneficial to the long term development of China's aircraft carrier capability than the short term deployment of the *Liaoning* for operations. The marginal gains from devoting the *Liaoning* for carrier focused research and training may outweigh the operational experience that the *Liaoning* may acquire if deployed for actual operations.

4. Research and training trumps all the other factors if the objective of the PLAN is to build a critical mass of talent, skills, knowledge and leadership to operate China's next generation of aircraft carriers. The pioneer crew and pilots of the *Liaoning* will not only need to excel in what they do, they will need to educate and train the next generation of carrier personnel. This will drain the resources of the first set of crew and may result in insufficient capacity to deploy the *Liaoning* for operations.

5. There is an urgency to focus on research and training because if China's intent is to build a credible carrier force, it will need to commence work on construction, shipbuilding and personnel training as soon as possible. However, this work cannot realistically commence unless the necessary research and study of the strengths and weaknesses of the carrier's systems are completed. Thus, there is an urgent need for comprehensive research to be performed on the *Liaoning*'s performance so that the next generation of carriers can take onboard all the recommendations.

Evidence inconsistent with H2's assertion that the *Liaoning* will only be used for research and training is as follows:

1. Research and training priorities can easily be superseded by operational concerns where national interests and pride are at stake. Unless the PLAN and Central Military Commission leadership have a clear and unambiguous understanding of the research and training priorities, the exigencies of serving the national interest will easily overcome such lofty goals.

2. The *Liaoning* was built as a warship for the PLAN, with the attendant weapon systems and highly trained and experienced crew. Unlike dedicated research and training platforms that may be unarmed and were obviously designed for such functions, the *Liaoning* was built for naval

operations. Thus, to expect that research and training will be long term priorities for the *Liaoning* is naïve.

Hypothesis 3: Consistent and Inconsistent Evidence and Arguments

There was little evidence in support of H3's assertion that the *Liaoning* will be an operational failure, unable to fulfill even its research and training role. While the *Liaoning* has obviously had its share of challenges trying to operationalize a challenging capability such as carrier aviation, there has not been any evidence to suggest that the *Liaoning* project may end in catastrophic failure.[191] In fact, evidence from China that the carrier's development program has its share of challenges suggests that the PLAN is not blind to the potential risks of developing *Liaoning*'s capabilities.[192] Apart from the absence of catastrophic failures with *Liaoning*'s development, the dearth of consistent evidence for H3 may also be a result of China's censorship of negative reports and unknown difficulties about *Liaoning*'s development. This possibility cannot be discounted so observers will need to be vigilant for negative reports. H3 will still be pursued for analysis to examine if evidence for H1 and H2 could have a possible impact on H3.

Evidence inconsistent with H3's assertion that the *Liaoning* will be an operational failure, unable to fulfill even its research and training role, is as follows:

1. The *Liaoning* has had a smooth transition from refurbishment to carrier flight trials. The PLAN appears to have a comprehensive plan for the development and enhancement of *Liaoning*'s capabilities that would minimize any catastrophic failure. The development of the *Liaoning* since its commissioning in September 2012 suggests that the *Liaoning*'s development is progressive and moving in the right direction for the PLAN.

2. Significant resources have been commitment for *Liaoning*'s development. While the magnitude of resource commitment does not directly reduce the risks associated with carrier development, it increases the probability of success. As more resources are committed within a functional and effective professional organization for the fulfillment of a goal, more mitigating measures and customized solutions can be implemented to

---

[191] David Axe, "China's Testing Woes Remind that Developing Carrier Planes is Hard," *Wired*, 21 March 2013, http://www.wired.com/dangerroom/2013/03/developing-warplanes-is-hard/.

[192] "Carrier Test Pilot Reveals: High Tempo Training Led Carrier's Arrestor Wire to Fail," Sina News 新浪军事 [China], 18 March 2013, http://mil.news.sina.com.cn/2013-03-18/0859718843.html.

facilitate success. An example is the *Liaoning*'s re-basing to a dedicated home base within the Qingdao naval base that took four years to construct.[193] Various land-based carrier flight training facilities like the facility in Wuhan also reduce the chance of catastrophic failure out at sea.[194] China's possible carrier catapult research facility demonstrates that considerable research and testing is performed before technology is fielded by the PLAN.[195]

3. China's Defense Ministry announced in April 2013 that the *Liaoning* was slated for a "high-seas voyage" within the year.[196] This announcement is a demonstration of the PLAN's confidence in the performance of the *Liaoning* and its availability and performance for a high-seas voyage that will likely be much publicized.

4. In April 2013, China announced that the PLAN's first carrier aviation unit was inaugurated.[197] Although the fact that the *Liaoning* had no dedicated organic aviation wing when it was commissioned in September 2012 became a source of ridicule for some foreign observers. The fact that China took careful and measured steps towards the building of such a demanding capability should instead give cause for concern. It is evident that China has given deliberate thought and planning towards the development of the *Liaoning* and is motivated to succeed even if more time and resources are required.

Step 3: Evidence Matrix for Comparison of Hypotheses

Step 3 of the ACH process calls for the construction of a matrix to compare the competing hypotheses against the assembled evidence from Step 2.[198] The purpose of Step 3 is to analyze the "diagnosticity" of the evidence and to determine which items of evidence are "most useful in judging the relative likelihood of alternative hypotheses."[199]

---

[193] Minnie Chan, "Carrier arrives at Qingdao home," *South China Morning Post*, 28 February 2013, 6.

[194] Godbole and Parmar, "China's Aircraft Carrier: Some Observations."

[195] John Reed, "Is this the prototype for China's first aircraft carrier catapult?" *Foreign Policy*, 28 March 2013, http://killerapps.foreignpolicy.com/posts/2013/03/28/is_this_the_prototype_for_chinas_first_aircraft_carrier_catapult.

[196] China's first carrier plans high-sea voyage," *Xinhua* (China), 19 April 2013, http://news.xinhuanet.com/english/china/2013-04/19/c_132323539.htm.

[197] "China forms its first carrier aviation unit," *People's Daily Online* (China), 11 May 2013.

[198] Heuer, *Psychology of Intelligence Analysis*, 100.

[199] Heuer, *Psychology of Intelligence Analysis*, 101.

In the matrix, the alphabet "C" indicates that a certain item of evidence is consistent with a particular hypothesis. The alphabet "I" indicates that a certain item of evidence is inconsistent with a particular hypothesis. If a particular piece of evidence indicates more consistency or inconsistency than others, a numerical value is added in front of the alphabet give it additional weight.

The type of evidence compiled for this case has been separated into three categories. "News" refers to evidence from open source news media that do not include official news media outlets from China. "China" refers to evidence from official news media outlets in China that are the government's mouthpieces. "Analyst" refers to opinions from external military domain experts and analysts including the authors of this paper.

Apart from listing the evidence and their correlation to the respective hypotheses, the matrix will evaluate the evidence on three criteria—Type, Credibility and Relevance. Type refers to the evidence type that is usually connected to the source of the evidence. Credibility measures the credibility of evidence that is normally linked to the credibility of the source. There are three degrees of credibility (high, medium and low) and the default is medium. Lastly, relevance measures how relevant particular evidence may be in relation to the issue being analyzed. There are three degrees of relevance (high, medium and low) and the default is medium. The ACH matrix is shown in Table 8 below.

The Competing Hypotheses regarding the *Liaoning*'s Role in the PLAN:

- H1 (Ops): *Liaoning* will spearhead operational deployment of China's aircraft carrier capability.

- H2 (R&D / Trng): *Liaoning* will be deployed for research and training purposes.

- H2 (Fail): *Liaoning* will be an operational failure, unable to fulfill even its research and training role.

Table 8.   ACH Matrix (First Iteration)

#	EVIDENCE	Evidence Type	Evidence Credibility	Relevance of Evidence	H1: Ops	H2: R&D / Trng	H3: Fail
	Weighted Inconsistency Score						
1	*Liaoning* touted as landmark of China's modernization of armed forces and national defense.	China	H	H	C	C	C
2	Transition from research and training to operational deployment easily achieved.	Analyst	M	H	C	C	I
3	*Liaoning* is a capable warship in its own right.	Analyst	M	M	C	C	I
4	*Liaoning* must hold the operational fort until other aircraft carriers are ready.	Analyst	M	H	2C	I	I
5	Restricting *Liaoning* to research and training is a waste of operational resources.	Analyst	M	M	C	I	I
6	*Liaoning* has significant operational value in East Asia.	Analyst	M	H	2C	I	I
7	Operational urgency may compel China to deploy *Liaoning* for operations.	Analyst	M	H	C	I	I
8	Strategic maritime plan was to deploy the aircraft carrier for force projection.	China	H	H	2C	I	I
9	*Liaoning* will not be ready for operational deployment.	Analyst	M	H	I	2C	C
10	One aircraft carrier is insufficient for sustainable operational deployment.	News	H	H	I	C	C
11	Deploying the *Liaoning* for operations would be too aggressive.	News	H	H	I	2C	I
12	Rest of PLAN may not be ready to support *Liaoning*.	News	H	H	I	2C	C
13	China wants the world to believe the *Liaoning* is only for research and training.	Analyst	M	M	I	C	I
14	Official position on the *Liaoning*'s role is that it serves research and training purposes.	China	M	H	I	C	I
15	Logical for research and training to be the *Liaoning*'s first priority.	China	M	M	I	C	I
16	Research and training is more beneficial to the long term development of China's carriers.	Analyst	M	M	I	C	I
17	Research and training trumps all the other factors if the objective of the PLAN is to build a critical mass of talent, skills, knowledge and leadership for next generation of aircraft carriers.	Analyst	M	M	I	C	C
18	Urgency to focus on research and training because China will need to commence work on construction, shipbuilding and personnel training for next generation of carriers soonest.	Analyst	M	H	I	C	C
19	Research and training priorities can be superseded by operational concerns.	Analyst	M	H	C	I	I
20	*Liaoning* was built as a warship for the PLAN, with the attendant weapon systems and highly trained and experienced crew.	Analyst	M	H	C	I	I

Continued on next page.

Continued from previous page.

		Analyst	Analyst	China	China
21	*Liaoning* had a smooth transition from refurbishment to carrier flight trials.	H	C	C	I
22	Significant resources have been commitment for *Liaoning*'s development.	M	C	C	I
23	*Liaoning* slated for a "high-seas voyage" to demonstrate its capability.	M	C	C	I
24	PLAN's first carrier aviation unit has been inaugurated.	M	C	C	I

101

a. Findings from Analysis of ACH Matrix (First Iteration)

Analysis of the initial comparison of the competing hypotheses with collated evidence offers the following insights:

1. <u>Evidence for H1 and H2 can overlap</u>. It appears that some evidence for H1 and H2 are either consistent or inconsistent for both hypotheses concurrently. This finding suggests that such evidence do not sufficiently make a distinction between H1 and H2.

2. <u>Evidence consistent for H1 and H2 are mostly inconsistent with H3</u>. Since H3 is predicated on the failure of both H1 and H2, most evidence that is consistent for H1 and H2 is inconsistent with H3. This is not unexpected as there was little evidence that was consistent with H3 to begin with. This finding strengthens the initial expectation during the formulation of H3 that it may be an unlikely result.

3. <u>Elimination of H3?</u> Given that the only evidence that is consistent with H3 is also compatible with H2 and lacks specific diagnosticity for H3, H3 was considered for elimination. However, there was no evidence that could disprove H3 conclusively. H3 simply remains unproven because there is a lack of diagnostic evidence, therefore it remains in consideration.

4. <u>Re-evaluation of evidence that is consistent with both H1 and H2</u>. To improve the diagnosticity of evidence for comparison, evidence that is consistent with both H1 and H2 will be re-evaluated for both hypotheses and re-examined. If the evidence continues to provide a lack of specific diagnosticity for either hypotheses, this evidence will be eliminated from consideration.

The findings from the initial analysis of the evidence matrix in Step 3 of ACH will be implemented in Step 4 of the ACH below.

Step 4: Refining the Evidence Matrix for Comparison of Hypotheses

To refine the presentation of evidence in the matrix, the evidence has been re-ordered, evidence with greater diagnosticity has been placed at the top, non-diagnostic evidence has been moved down. In addition, evidence with greater sensitivity based on their credibility and relevance has also been moved up. This allows for clearer analysis of diagnostic evidence that is sensitive to the hypotheses.

a. Reassessment of Evidence Diagnosticity.

The following evidence in Table 9 was consistent with both H1 and H2. They will be re-evaluated to improve their respective diagnosticity for either H1 or H2.

Table 9.   Evidence consistent with both H1 and H2.

		H1: Ops	H2: R&D / Trng	H3: Fail
2	Transition from research and training to operational deployment easily achieved.	C	C	I
3	*Liaoning* is a capable warship in its own right.	C	C	I
21	*Liaoning* had a smooth transition from refurbishment to carrier flight trials.	C	C	I
22	Significant resources have been commitment for *Liaoning*'s development.	C	C	I
23	*Liaoning* slated for a "high-seas voyage" to demonstrate its capability.	C	C	I
24	PLAN's first carrier aviation unit has been inaugurated.	C	C	I

1.   <u>Transition from research and training to operational deployment is easily achieved</u>. Upon closer examination, this evidence is actually more consistent for H1 than H2. This is because even if the *Liaoning* could be used for research and training, it is the ease with which it can be converted for operational deployment that is critical to our analysis. The fact that it can be easily deployed for operations as well weighs the evidence in favor of H1 and against H2.

2.   <u>*Liaoning* is a capable warship in its own right</u>. Since the *Liaoning* is a capable warship on its own, that makes it even more likely to be deployed for operations as opposed to just research and training. There will be a greater temptation for policy makers to employ it in operations and there will be fewer obstacles to it being so deployed. Therefore this evidence is weighed in favor of H1 and against H2.

3.   <u>*Liaoning* had a smooth transition from refurbishment to carrier flight trials</u>. The smooth transition from refurbishment to carrier flight trials should come down in favor of H1 because it is likely to lead to a greater propensity to deploy the *Liaoning* for operations. In fact, the smoother the developments and enhancements to the *Liaoning*, the greater is the likelihood that the carrier will be deployed for operations. After all, the purpose of research and training is to improve operations. For the same reason, the inauguration of the PLAN's first carrier aviation unit will also be considered as evidence in favor of H1.

4.   <u>*Liaoning* slated for a "high-seas voyage" to demonstrate its capability</u>. Even though the details of the high-seas voyage have not been announced, the declaration and the nature of the voyage points towards a desire to demonstrate *Liaoning*'s capability in a regional tour de force. Such a motivation must come down in favor of H1 since a demonstration of potential force is only credible if that force can be operationalized with ease.

The re-evaluated diagnostics for the ambiguous evidence is presented in Table 10:

Table 10.   Re-evaluated evidence consistent with both H1 and H2.

		H1: Ops	H2: R&D / Trng	H3: Fail
2	Transition from research and training to operational deployment easily achieved.	2C	C	I
3	*Liaoning* is a capable warship in its own right.	2C	C	I
21	*Liaoning* had a smooth transition from refurbishment to carrier flight trials.	2C	C	I
22	Significant resources have been commitment for *Liaoning*'s development.	2C	C	I
23	*Liaoning* slated for a "high-seas voyage" to demonstrate its capability.	2C	C	I
24	PLAN's first carrier aviation unit has been inaugurated.	2C	C	I

b. **Value of Evidence Inconsistent with Hypotheses**.

One of the advantages of using the ACH is the consideration of inconsistent evidence. Heuer explained that the failings of many intelligence analyses are caused by over-emphasis on consistent evidence and insufficient attention on inconsistent evidence.[200] Consistent data can often support more than one hypothesis and inconsistent data can prove to be of greater value in disproving particular hypotheses than consistent data in proving them. The other pitfall with consistent evidence is that analysts will naturally look for consistent evidence to support their hunches and preferred hypotheses rather than seeking inconsistent evidence to disprove their preferred hypotheses. Lastly, the adversary who employs deception will plant evidence to mislead the intelligence analyst and steer him towards a hypothesis preferred by the enemy. This means that evidence consistent with a particular hypothesis may be planted by the adversary to lead one towards the hypothesis that the enemy wants him to believe.

To account for the evidence that is inconsistent with the hypotheses, a "weighted inconsistency score" will be calculated for each hypotheses based on the Credibility, Relevance and degree of Inconsistency for each piece of relevant evidence. Every piece of inconsistent evidence will be assigned a score relevant to its hypothesis and the total "weighted inconsistency score" for each hypothesis will be compiled. The "weighted inconsistency score" will be derived from the weighted inconsistency counting algorithm shown in Table 11 below that assigns a score based on the interaction of three values: Credibility, Relevance and degree of Inconsistency.[201]

---

[200] Heuer, *Psychology of Intelligence Analysis,* 104.

[201] The Weighted Inconsistency Counting algorithm was developed by the Naval Postgraduate School's Hy Rothstein to improve the utility of Richards Heuer's Analysis of Competitive Hypotheses.

Table 11.   Weighted Inconsistency Counting Algorithm

Credibility	Relevance	Inconsistency (I)	Inconsistency - significant (2I)
High (H)	High (H)	2	4
Medium (M)	High (H)	1.414	2.828
Low (L)	High (H)	1	2
High (H)	Medium (M)	1.414	2.828
Medium (M)	Medium (M)	1	2
Low (L)	Medium (M)	0.707	1.414
High (H)	Low (L)	1	2
Medium (M)	Low (L)	0.705	1.414
Low (L)	Low (L)	0.5	1

Therefore, the refined ACH matrix is as presented in Table 12.

Table 12.   ACH Matrix (Second Iteration)

	EVIDENCE	Evidence Type	Evidence Credibility	Relevance of Evidence	H1: Ops	H2: R&D / Trng	H3: Fail
	Weighted Inconsistency Score				14.242	10.07	18.484
8	Strategic maritime plan was to deploy the aircraft carrier for force projection.	China	H	H	2C	I	I
10	One aircraft carrier is insufficient for sustainable operational deployment.	News	H	H	I	C	C
11	Deploying the *Liaoning* for operations would be too aggressive.	News	H	H	I	2C	I
12	Rest of PLAN may not be ready to support *Liaoning*.	News	H	H	I	2C	C
4	*Liaoning* must hold the operational fort until other aircraft carriers are ready.	Analyst	M	H	2C	I	I
6	*Liaoning* has significant operational value in East Asia.	Analyst	M	H	2C	I	I
7	Operational urgency may compel China to deploy *Liaoning* for operations.	Analyst	M	H	C	I	C
9	*Liaoning* will not be ready for operational deployment.	Analyst	M	H	I	2C	I
14	Official position on the *Liaoning*'s role is that it serves research and training purposes.	China	M	H	I	C	I
18	Urgency to focus on research and training because China will need to commence work on construction, shipbuilding and personnel training for next generation of carriers soonest.	Analyst	M	H	I	C	C
19	Research and training priorities can be superseded by operational concerns.	Analyst	M	H	C	I	I
20	*Liaoning* was built as a warship for the PLAN, with the attendant weapon systems and highly trained and experienced crew.	Analyst	M	H	C	I	I
5	Restricting *Liaoning* to research and training is a waste of operational resources.	Analyst	M	M	C	I	I
13	China wants the world to believe the *Liaoning* is only for research and training.	Analyst	M	M	I	C	I
15	Logical for research and training to be the *Liaoning*'s first priority.	China	M	M	I	C	I
16	Research and training is more beneficial to the long term development of China's carriers.	Analyst	M	M	I	C	I
17	Research and training trumps all the other factors if the objective of the PLAN is to build a critical mass of talent, skills, knowledge and leadership for next generation of aircraft carriers.	Analyst	M	M	I	C	C
21	*Liaoning* had a smooth transition from refurbishment to carrier flight trials.	Analyst	H	M	2C	C	I
22	Significant resources have been commitment for *Liaoning*'s development.	Analyst	M	M	2C	C	I
23	*Liaoning* slated for a "high-seas voyage" to demonstrate its capability.	China	M	M	2C	C	I
24	PLAN's first carrier aviation unit has been inaugurated.	China	M	M	2C	C	I
2	Transition from research and training to operational deployment easily achieved.	Analyst	M	H	2C	C	I

Continued on next page.

Continued from previous page.

		Analyst	M	M	2C	C	I
		China	H	H	C	C	C
3	*Liaoning* is a capable warship in its own right.						
1	*Liaoning* touted as landmark of China's modernization of armed forces and national defense.						

107

a. Findings from Analysis of Evidence Matrix for Competing Hypotheses

1. Evidence for H1 and H2 are evenly matched. Considering both consistent and inconsistent evidence for H1 and H2, they appear to be quite evenly matched across the spectrum of evidence. The bottom third of the matrix also suggests that there is significant evidence that appears to be consistent across both hypotheses. This finding suggests that H1 and H2 are evenly matched, and it may even be hard to distinguish one from the other. This is not surprising as the difference between operational activities and research /training activities can be difficult to distinguish especially in peacetime and at the early stages of a new military capability like an aircraft carrier's evolution when many dual purpose activities may be ongoing. This also suggests that it could be easy for China to disguise some operational activity as training activity.

2. H3 is very unlikely. H3 has very little evidence that is consistent and the highest weighted inconsistency score of 18.484 among the three hypotheses. This finding is not surprising given the initial expectations and the weight of evidence against H3. Thus, although H3 cannot be disproved, its likelihood is the least among the three hypotheses considered. This would leave the ACH process as a two-horse race between H1 and H2.

3. Removal of non-diagnostic evidence from consideration. Some of the non-diagnostic evidence in the bottom third of the matrix that are consistent across both H1 and H2 will be removed in the next iteration of the ACH matrix to allow for greater focus on more diagnostic evidence.

4. Relevant evidence that is missing. When examining H1 and the evidence compiled thus far, there appears to be relevant evidence that is missing. Additional evidence that may indicate that the *Liaoning* will be deployed for operations are described below and will be included as additional evidence in the next iteration of the ACH matrix.

    i. Evidence of *Liaoning*'s basing near possible areas of operation. Is the *Liaoning* being located nearer to possible operational areas? Its new base in Qingdao is the headquarters of the North Sea Fleet and it appears that the *Liaoning*'s basing there instead of farther east with the East Sea Fleet or farther south with the South Sea Fleet is ostensibly to impress external observers that the *Liaoning* should not be seen as a threat to the region.[202] A more practical reason is that it would be easier for the integration and training of carrier-based aircraft being based out of *Liaoning* province. At the same time, the construction of a large new naval base at Yulin on Hainan Island farther south and existing bases do not preclude the possibility that the *Liaoning* may be relocated farther east or south when it is ready for operations.

---

[202] Christian Le Miere, "Why China sent its aircraft carrier to Qingdao," *International Institute for Strategic Studies*, 7 March 2013, http://www.iiss.org/en/iiss%20voices/blogsections/iiss-voices-2013-1e35/march-2013-6eb6/china-aircraft-carrier-1bb4.

ii.   <u>Build-up of a possible carrier task force</u>. Are there signs that a new carrier task force is being built up for possible operation with the *Liaoning*? The PLAN is Asia's largest Navy and operates modern warships of the type that can be deployed as part of an aircraft carrier task force. China reported that the PLAN's ships have been conducting concerted training in preparation for aircraft carrier task force operations and mentioned a five to ten year horizon to realize the carrier task force's full operational capabilities.[203] Thus, it is not inconceivable that ships may be assigned for carrier task force operations in the future.

5.   <u>Preponderance of evidence consistent with H2</u>. Due to the fact that the *Liaoning* is a new capability for the PLAN and significant components of it (like the carrier air wing) are still being developed, there will be a preponderance of evidence consistent with H2 rather than H1. The danger in discounting H1 lies in the fact that training and research are phases that all military capabilities must go through to achieve operational status. The question with the *Liaoning* is whether its role ends with training and research or does it go beyond that to actual operations. China would like us to believe the former even as it prepares for the latter. We have to be aware of this as we consider each hypothesis and its relevant evidence.

Step 5: Draw Tentative Conclusions about the Likelihood of Each Hypothesis

After considering evidence against respective hypothesis, Heuer recommends examining each hypothesis as a whole in Step 5 of ACH with the objective of trying to disprove them.[204] This is to avoid the pitfall of assigning more weight of consistent evidence to a preferred hypothesis instead of examining critical evidence that refutes it. For this, the weighted inconsistency score of each hypothesis will be critical to assessing their plausibility. The updated ACH matrix is shown as shown in Table 13.

The Competing Hypotheses regarding the *Liaoning*'s Role in the PLAN:

- H1 (Ops): *Liaoning* will spearhead operational deployment of China's aircraft carrier capability.

- H2 (R&D / Trng): *Liaoning* will be deployed for research and training purposes.

- H2 (Fail): *Liaoning* will be an operational failure, unable to fulfill even its research and training role.

---

[203] Tao Hai, "PLA Navy makes preparations for aircraft carrier formation," *Xinhua* (China), 13 December 2012, http://eng.chinamil.com.cn/news-channels/china-military-news/2012-12/13/content_5140986.htm.

[204] Heuer, *Psychology of Intelligence Analysis,* 104.

Table 13.   ACH Matrix (Third Iteration)

	EVIDENCE	Evidence Type	Evidence Credibility	Relevance of Evidence	H1: Ops	H2: R&D / Trng	H3: Fail
	Weighted Inconsistency Score				16.242	12.07	20.484
8	Strategic maritime plan was to deploy the aircraft carrier for force projection.	China	H	H	2C	I	I
10	One aircraft carrier is insufficient for sustainable operational deployment.	News	H	H	I	C	C
11	Deploying the *Liaoning* for operations would be too aggressive.	News	H	H	I	2C	I
12	Rest of PLAN may not be ready to support *Liaoning*.	News	H	H	I	2C	C
25	Build up of possible carrier task force.	China	H	H	2C	I	I
26	Basing of *Liaoning* with North Sea Fleet in Qingdao.	China	H	H	I	C	I
4	*Liaoning* must hold the operational fort until other aircraft carriers are ready.	Analyst	M	H	2C	I	I
6	*Liaoning* has significant operational value in East Asia.	Analyst	M	H	2C	I	I
7	Operational urgency may compel China to deploy *Liaoning* for operations.	Analyst	M	H	C	I	I
9	*Liaoning* will not be ready for operational deployment.	Analyst	M	H	I	2C	C
14	Official position on the *Liaoning*'s role is that it serves research and training purposes.	China	M	H	I	C	I
18	Urgency to focus on research and training because China will need to commence work on construction, shipbuilding and personnel training for next generation of carriers soonest.	Analyst	M	H	I	C	C
19	Research and training priorities can be superseded by operational concerns.	Analyst	M	H	C	I	I
20	*Liaoning* was built as a warship for the PLAN, with the attendant weapon systems and highly trained and experienced crew.	Analyst	M	H	C	I	I
5	Restricting *Liaoning* to research and training is a waste of operational resources.	Analyst	M	M	C	I	I
13	China wants the world to believe the *Liaoning* is only for research and training.	Analyst	M	M	I	C	I
15	Logical for research and training to be the *Liaoning*'s first priority.	China	M	M	I	C	I
16	Research and training is more beneficial to the long term development of China's carriers.	Analyst	M	M	I	C	I
17	Research and training trumps all the other factors if the objective of the PLAN is to build a critical mass of talent, skills, knowledge and leadership for next generation of aircraft carriers.	Analyst	M	M	I	C	C

a. Findings from Analysis of Evidence Matrix for Competing Hypotheses

1.   <u>Weighted Inconsistency Scores</u>. To Heuer, the presence of less contradictory evidence for a particular hypothesis was more critical than the presence of more supporting evidence because supporting evidence could be consistent with other hypotheses that were not taken into consideration.[205] The weighted inconsistency scores for each hypothesis measure the extent of inconsistent evidence for each hypothesis. H3 still has the highest score of 20.484, followed by H1 at 16.242 and H2 at 12.07. It appears that H3 is the most unlikely hypothesis and H2 the most likely one since it has the lowest score of inconsistent evidence. Although H2 has the lowest inconsistency score, we shall discuss why H1 should be examined farther.

2.   <u>Inconsistency score for H1 higher than H2</u>. Although the inconsistency score for H1 is higher than H2, there is room for greater analysis for why that is the case. A major contributor to H1's high inconsistency score is H1's inconsistent evidence that have both high credibility and high relevance. These four sensitive items of evidence are:

10	One aircraft carrier is insufficient for sustainable operational deployment.
11	Deploying the *Liaoning* for operations would be too aggressive.
12	Rest of PLAN may not be ready to support *Liaoning*.
26	Basing of *Liaoning* with North Sea Fleet in Qingdao.

3.   If any one of these sensitive evidence changes in consistency, the weighted inconsistency scores of both H1 and H2 will be significantly affected and achieve near parity. In Step 6 of the ACH, the implications of changes in these items of critical evidence will be elaborated.

4.   <u>H2 as the least inconsistent hypothesis</u>. With the lowest weighted inconsistency score, H2 is the most likely of the three hypotheses. This means that the outcome of our analysis of competitive hypotheses has yielded an outcome that is congruent with China's official version of the *Liaoning*'s purpose. Cognizant of the possibility of China's manipulation of evidence to favor an impression that the *Liaoning*'s role is for training and research, we should accept this initial finding with an eye for re-evaluation at a later date as developments in China's carrier development continue. This early phase of the *Liaoning*'s development may also result in evidence favoring a training and research role, as the *Liaoning* matures, this assessment must be re-evaluated.

---

[205] Heuer, *Psychology of Intelligence Analysis*, 104.

Therefore the tentative conclusion is that H2 is the most likely among the three hypotheses—the *Liaoning* will be deployed for research and training purposes.

Step 6: Analysis of Conclusion for Sensitivity to Critical Evidence

Step 6 of the ACH calls for the examination of the conclusion arrived at Step 5 with critical pieces of evidence that may significantly alter the conclusion if the evidence was wrong or misleading. At this stage, we want to question if there were questionable assumptions that have led us to this particular conclusion. Could incomplete evidence have misled us to make an erroneous conclusion? Are there alternative explanations that fit the same evidence considered?

Evidence critical to H2 have been highlighted in yellow in Table 14 and will be examined in detail.

Table 14.   Review of ACH Matrix (Third Iteration)

		Type	Cred-ibility	Relev-ance	H1: Ops	H2: R&D/ Trng	H3: Fail
	Weighted Inconsistency Score				16.2	12.07	20.4
	EVIDENCE						
8	Strategic maritime plan was to deploy the aircraft carrier for force projection.	China	H	H	2C	I	I
10	One aircraft carrier is insufficient for sustainable operational deployment.	News	H	H	I	C	C
11	Deploying the *Liaoning* for operations would be too aggressive.	News	H	H	I	2C	I
12	Rest of PLAN may not be ready to support *Liaoning*.	News	H	H	I	2C	C
25	Build up of possible carrier task force.	China	H	H	2C	I	I
26	Basing of *Liaoning* with North Sea Fleet in Qingdao.	China	H	H	I	C	I
4	*Liaoning* must hold the operational fort until other aircraft carriers are ready.	Analyst	M	H	2C	I	I
6	*Liaoning* has significant operational value in East Asia.	Analyst	M	H	2C	I	I
7	Operational urgency may compel China to deploy *Liaoning* for operations.	Analyst	M	H	C	I	I
	Continued on next page.						
	Continued from previous page.						
9	*Liaoning* will not be ready for operational deployment.	Analyst	M	H	I	2C	C
14	Official position on the *Liaoning*'s role is that it serves research and training purposes.	China	M	H	I	C	I
18	Urgency to focus on research and training because China will need to commence work on construction, shipbuilding and personnel training for next generation of carriers soonest.	Analyst	M	H	I	C	C
19	Research and training priorities can be superseded by operational concerns.	Analyst	M	H	C	I	I
20	*Liaoning* was built as a warship for the PLAN, with the attendant weapon systems and highly trained and experienced crew.	Analyst	M	H	C	I	I
5	Restricting *Liaoning* to research and training is a waste of operational resources.	Analyst	M	M	C	I	I
13	China wants the world to believe the *Liaoning* is only for research and training.	Analyst	M	M	I	C	I
15	Logical for research and training to be the *Liaoning*'s first priority.	China	M	M	I	C	I
16	Research and training is more beneficial to the long term development of China's carriers.	Analyst	M	M	I	C	I
17	Research and training trumps all the other factors if the objective of the PLAN is to build a critical mass of talent, skills, knowledge and leadership for next generation of aircraft carriers.	Analyst	M	M	I	C	C

a. Examination of Critical Evidence

- **Delicate Balance of Weighted Inconsistency Scores between H1 and H2.** If the weighted inconsistency scores of H1 and H2 are pivotal to our judgment of which is the most likely hypothesis, we must consider how close their separation actually is when considering the impact of critical evidence. The high credibility and high relevance critical evidence of H2 have been highlighted in yellow in Table 7 above. If any _one_ of these four items of evidence turns out to be inconsistent, the weighted inconsistency scores between H1 and H2 would almost be equal—14.242 for H1 and 14.07 for H2. This highlights the sensitivity of the weighted inconsistency scores to the critical evidence. As alluded to in the findings of Step 5 of the ACH, the possibility that these critical items of evidence may change cannot be ruled out. We discuss these four items of critical evidence next.

- **Critical Consistent Evidence for H2.** The first of these is the assertion that one aircraft carrier is insufficient for sustainable operational deployment. While this operating constraint remains true, it does not preclude the possibility that the _Liaoning_ may be deployed for one-off limited operations should the need arise. Prolonged deployments of the _Liaoning_ should not be the only definition of its operational use.

  The second critical inconsistent evidence for H1 is that deploying the _Liaoning_ for operations may be perceived as being too aggressive for China's narrative about peaceful development. Perceptions about acceptable levels of aggressiveness can change quickly with circumstances and the possibility that operational deployment of the _Liaoning_ would not be perceived by China as aggressive should not be totally discounted. China's 2013 statement on the legitimacy of its patrols in disputed waters in the South and East China Seas gives credence to the possibility that the _Liaoning_'s deployment may not necessarily be perceived as aggressive by China in the long term.[206]

  The third critical inconsistent evidence for H1 claims that the rest of the PLAN may not be ready to support the _Liaoning_'s deployment is possibly subject to rapid change. The PLAN is a large navy and it is not inconceivable that its naval assets may be re-organized to support the _Liaoning_ for operations. There are already signs that the PLAN is preparing for carrier task force operations so the possibility of _Liaoning_'s deployment cannot be definitively ruled out.[207]

---

[206] "China patrols in Asian seas 'legitimate': General," _Agence France-Presse_, 2 June 2013, http://www.afp.com/en/news/topstories/chinese-patrols-asian-seas-legitimate-general/.

[207] Tao Hai, "PLA Navy makes preparations for aircraft carrier formation."

Last, the deployment of the *Liaoning* to the North Sea Fleet in Qingdao should not be taken as a long term move. The *Liaoning*'s current deployment to Qingdao facilitates the integration of its fledging carrier air wing onboard. However, should the operational need arise, it is possible that the *Liaoning* may be stationed farther south at the newly constructed naval base in Yulin on Hainan Island that is 2,500km closer to the South China Sea; or farther East in Ningbo that is 1000km closer to the East China Sea.[208]

- It is assessed that H2 is sensitive to the critical evidence identified above. It is also noted that three out of the four critical items of evidence are essentially assumptions made about China's military capabilities and posture. Apart from the fact that China has only one operational aircraft carrier, the other items of evidence are not based on the presence or absence of physical specimens, but projections of China's behavior. This makes the critical evidence subject to major changes from the influence of politics, leadership personalities and geopolitics. The fickle nature of the critical evidence is both its strength (for its explanatory power) and weakness (for its potential ephemerality).

Step 7: Conclusions and Likelihood of All Hypotheses

This thesis will not be providing a statistical probability for each hypothesis. It will instead rank the hypotheses by three broad categories that are not quantified numerically but that provide a narrative assessment of each hypothesis. Heuer advocated the consideration of alternate hypotheses even after their evaluation in earlier steps because it is important to consider why alternative hypotheses are assessed to be weaker and therefore rejected.[209]

Hypothesis 1 (H1) postulates that the *Liaoning* will spearhead the operational deployment of China's aircraft carrier capability. H1 provides a realistic assessment of the *Liaoning*'s role based on the *Liaoning*'s envisaged capabilities, the scarcity of alternate options to the *Liaoning* and the manipulative nature of China's strategic ethos. Based on the analysis of competitive hypotheses, H1 is assessed to be the second most likely hypothesis among the three. It was ranked lower than H2 because its weighted

---

[208] Christian Le Miere, "Why China sent its aircraft carrier to Qingdao."

[209] Heuer, *Psychology of Intelligence Analysis,* 107.

inconsistency score was higher than H2's. However, in light of the sensitivity of the evidence dividing H1 and H2, it is advised that observers continue to evaluate the developing situation as the chances of the evidence turning in favor of H1 are significant.

Hypothesis 2 (H2) postulates that the *Liaoning* will serve limited research and training roles. H2 is an idealistic assessment of the *Liaoning*'s role that is encouraged by China but it underweights the importance of political and military realities and their effects on the *Liaoning*'s role in the PLAN. H2 provides expedient political and military cover for China's development of the *Liaoning*. As the delineation between training and operations is not always clear, the evidence in support of H2 is susceptible to manipulation by China. Based on the analysis of competitive hypothesis, H2 is currently the most likely hypothesis of the three. Its weighted inconsistency score is the lowest. Although it has been assessed to be the most likely hypothesis, the sensitive nature of the critical evidence in support of H2 is susceptible to drastic change. Thus, the *Liaoning*'s development must be monitored and updates to the evidence should be evaluated against the hypotheses when appropriate.

Hypothesis 3 (H3): The *Liaoning* will be an operational failure, unable to fulfill even its roles in research and training. H3 exemplifies wishful thinking from China's opponents and exceedingly pessimistic estimates by *Liaoning*'s detractors. The acquisition and development of the *Liaoning* has demonstrated careful planning and implementation of strategy and policy by China—attributes that are likely to pre-empt catastrophic failures rather than precipitate them. H3 is the least likely of the three hypotheses and is very unlikely compared with H1 and H2. Its weighted inconsistency score is the highest of the three. Although it is the least likely of the three hypotheses, it has not been disproved so it remains an outside possibility.

Step 8: Milestones for Observation and Reassessment

Step 8 takes the analysis and the conclusion regarding the most likely hypothesis a farther step into the future by identifying milestones for observation of evidence that may be consistent or inconsistent with the current assessments. Heuer advised that "analytical conclusions should always be tentative" because reality may change in ways that affect postulated appraisals of a situation.[210] By identifying in advance the kind of evidence that would cause the analyst to reconsider his evaluation and reassess the situation, Heuer believes we can pre-empt the human tendency to rationalize away future developments as inconsequential and irrelevant to potential modifications of earlier judgements.[211]

Given the assessment that H2 is most likely, and the sensitive nature of the critical evidence relevant to that assessment, the following milestones are assessed to be significant and relevant to the continued validity of H2's likelihood and changes in them should be reasons for reassessment of the conclusions about the *Liaoning*'s role in the PLAN.

1. Operationalization of the carrier fighter wing onboard the *Liaoning* for regular flight operations at sea. This would represent a major developmental milestone for the *Liaoning*, undermine H2 and strengthen the likelihood of H1.

2. Deployment of the *Liaoning* for any type of operation that is beyond research and training. Regardless of what sort of capabilities the *Liaoning* may be deployed with, its deployment for operations would set a precedent that increases the likelihood that it will be deployed again. Deployment of *Liaoning* for any operations will disprove H2.

3. Major incidents that are detrimental to the development of the *Liaoning*, e.g. significant accidents, damage to the ship, loss of confidence in the ability of the carrier, loss of funding etc. Such incidents would retard the *Liaoning*'s development and result in a backlash that would likely result in a more conservative approach to *Liaoning*'s development and deployment. Such negative incidents would strengthen H2 and H3 and weaken H1.

4. Major developments that result in the usurpation of the *Liaoning*'s roles like the commissioning of new carriers in the PLAN, or new operational concepts that render the *Liaoning*'s roles redundant, like the construction of new airbases in the South or East China Sea that extend the air coverage of China's land based aircraft. Such incidents would weaken H1. The oddity would then be that the *Liaoning* may no longer be the vessel for projecting China's influence, some other platform or capability would take its place.

---

[210] Heuer, *Psychology of Intelligence Analysis,* 108.

[211] Heuer, *Psychology of Intelligence Analysis,* 108.

D. CONCLUSION

This chapter has attempted to postulate what the *Liaoning*'s role in the PLAN will be. This inquiry is a natural progression from the study about the acquisition and refurbishment of China's first aircraft carrier. Although the assessment has been made that the *Liaoning* will most likely be deployed for training and research at this phase of its development, this assessment is by no means final and is subject to revision based on actual developments of the *Liaoning*'s capabilities. The alternate hypotheses H1 and H3 have not been disproven, they merely remain unproven and may yet come to pass. Important developmental milestones have been identified for continued assessment of competing hypotheses in the future.

VIII. CONCLUSION

This thesis set out to explain the motivation and method behind China's employment of deception in the acquisition and development of its first aircraft carrier, the *Liaoning*. This task was accomplished by examining the following key areas of significance to the *Liaoning* deception:

- China's strategic psyche and its relation to deception
- China's national goals and strategy that drove its interest in the maritime arena
- China's maritime goals and strategy that motivated the acquisition of an aircraft carrier
- The PLA Navy's heritage and its influence on China's naval development
- China's employment of strategic deception
- Details of the *Liaoning* acquisition and development

The approach was to first seek a broad understanding of China and its culture towards deception; then its motivations and strategies; and finally its methods and implementation efforts. It was a story about the Chinese navy's evolution from a fledging coastal force to the largest navy in Asia today—one that is on the precipice of joining the ranks of blue water naval powers like the United States. The main actor of our slice of China's naval story was the former Soviet aircraft carrier, the *Varyag*, which was given a new lease of life through the classic Chinese deception concept of "reviving a corpse" and reincarnating the *Varyag* as the *Liaoning*—the pride of the PLAN fleet today and the most visible symbol of China's maritime ambitions for East Asia.

The thesis also assessed the likely role of the *Liaoning* in the PLAN after its commissioning in September 2012. We believed that China's stratagem with the *Liaoning* did not culminate at its commissioning. China has continued to deceive by pulling a veil over the *Liaoning*'s obvious purpose as a power-projecting aircraft carrier. Instead, China insisted that the *Liaoning*'s capabilities were far from complete, that it would require more time and resources to build a competent carrier force and therefore the *Liaoning* would focus on training and research, insinuating that operations were not the *Liaoning*'s primary function. We investigated whether China's assertions about the *Liaoning*'s role were truthful or deceitful.

A. FINDINGS OF THE STUDY

The study of the *Liaoning* deception revealed the following:

1. China's deception regarding the acquisition and development of the *Liaoning* was rational in its motivation, complex in its planning, simple in execution, patient in perspective and highly effective despite its bluff being called on more than one occasion. It was not a one-off fluke because it was the result of a series of conscious and calculated decisions.

2. China's deception management was skillfully executed after the *Liaoning* deception was underway to maximize the desired effects of deception even after its bluff was called. With its desired objectives driving its stratagem, China implemented various mitigating measures and behaviors to ensure the success of the deception ploy.

3. China effectively exploited foreign perceptions about its alleged weaknesses. It allowed China to reinforce under-estimation of its own capabilities and obfuscate its ultimate goals for the *Varyag*. Apart from active measures to shape perceptions about its intentions and ability, China took reactive measures targeted at independent reports that allowed it to exploit the attention directed towards the *Varyag* for further deception. Even after China's declaration of carrier construction in 2011, estimates of the carrier's launch dates were well off the mark—pointing to China's success in deceiving foreign intelligence estimates of its aircraft carrier development efforts for more than a decade.

4. China was unapologetic about its employment of deception regarding the *Liaoning* and saw its success as a strategic victory to be celebrated. China considered its disingenuous positions on the *Varyag*'s development as sophisticated strategic maneuvering and did not feel obliged to express remorse or provide any ex-post facto explanation. After the *Liaoning*'s commissioning, China's silence on justifications for its misleading statements, actions and positions about the *Varyag* reinforces the belief that the bodyguard of lies surrounding its first aircraft carrier has not been lifted. It also demonstrates the value of not disclosing one's employment of deception even after objectives have been achieved because it then perpetuates the various doubts in the mind of the adversary, leaves him open to further deception and gives his inferior strategic state of cognizance no relief.

5. China had no qualms about deceiving its own population as part of the *Liaoning* deception and in fact exploited its own population as part of the

ruse to provide cover for the *Varyag*. By employing the *Minsk* and *Kiev* as highly visible lures to direct attention away from the *Varyag*, China exploited its own populace by employing them as unknowing participants through commercialization of the *Minsk* and *Kiev* entertainment theme parks. When the *Varyag* failed to materialize in Macau and became a long term resident of Dalian's shipyards, China never saw a need to explain this alteration of plan.

6. There was no discernible start or finish for China's employment of strategic deception. It was a continuous and purposeful balancing of truth and deceit that was fluid and amorphous. Even after the *Liaoning* was commissioned, the deception ploy did not just "end." It presumably entered another phase to downplay the *Liaoning*'s operational importance and influence foreign perceptions about the capability and operational relevance of the *Liaoning*.

7. Western principles and values leave them susceptible to China's deception ploys which are tailored for maximum effectiveness against the target audience. The West operates on the basis of truth, while China operates on more than just the truth—to include uninformative silence, half-truths that confuse and outright deceit. China does not perceive such behavior as dishonest or demeaning. Deception that serves strategic outcomes vital to the national interest is not just accepted but expected of Chinese strategists. Success is attributed to astute strategic scheming and recognized as strategic excellence. China does not employ deception to humiliate its adversaries; it uses deception as a legitimate method to pursue tangible national interests. In other words, when employing deception, China does not mean to give offense. Therefore, the targets of its deception should take no offense in being deceived because strategic deception is not personal, it is merely part of national strategy.

B. IMPLICATIONS OF THE FINDINGS

The implications of our findings can serve to educate policy makers and analysts in understanding and dealing with China's propensity to employ deception. Consider the following:

1. Assume that China will employ strategic deception in pursuit of its national interests. It is critical to consider if deception will serve China's national interests, because if it does not, there is no motivation to use deception. Deceiving others without clear strategic interests does not serve China's national interests.

121

2. Do not expect China to come clean about its deception ploys or admit that its bluff has been called. Deception is considered a part of China's strategic calculus, and since there is no clear or fixed boundary on matters of national strategy, China will keep its options open by not admitting to deception or providing information to suggest than deception was even employed. Even if its bluff is called, China will likely respond with a poker face, because in a strategic game, the end remains flexible. Creating doubt is easier as long as no admission is made.

3. China facilitates the under-estimation by opponents of its capabilities because it is cognizant of Sun Tzu's guidance that:

He who has a thorough knowledge of his conditions as well as the enemy's conditions is sure to win all battles. He who has a thorough knowledge of his conditions but not the conditions of the enemy has an even chance of winning or losing a battle. He who has neither a knowledge of his own condition nor of the enemy's is sure to lose in every battle.[212]

Contrary to the Western concept of deterrence through the exhibition of force and capability, providing lesser indications of one's strength is meant to lull the opponent into a false sense of security and to cultivate over-confidence in the opponent's estimates of himself. Thus, when making estimates of China's capabilities, one must consider deception designed to make an opponent under-estimate their true capabilities and intentions.

4. China's strategic competitors should not feel affronted by China's employment of deception because it is part of their strategy psyche. China employs deception not to demean but to pursue national interests. This is important because if countries feel affronted by Chinese deception and prematurely close negotiations or dialogues, they may be shortchanging themselves of more beneficial outcomes from continued engagement of China. Instead, countries should continue to engage China and even employ deception against the Chinese to gain strategic parity or advantage over them.

5. Employ strong intelligence analysis tools to analyze evidence in areas of interest and to reduce the effectiveness of deception. Relevant agencies and analysts need to be educated about the analytical tools that exist to investigate evidence and compare hypotheses so that deception can be properly identified during the intelligence analysis process. Richards J. Heuer's Analysis of Competitive Hypothesis is an excellent analytical tool.

---

[212] Yu, *Sun Tzu on the Art of War*, 71.

6.   Do not take China's statements at face value. Look beyond ostensible facts and evidence. Give thought to what is *not* being said as much as what is said. In the spirit of Heuer's suspicion of consistent evidence, seek evidence that is inconsistent with hypotheses assumed to be true, as consistent evidence is insufficient to confirm the veracity of hypotheses. Consistent evidence may be an indicator of successful deception by the adversary who would provide consistent evidence supporting a hypothesis that the adversary wants us to believe. With such knowledge and skills, we can uncover deception.

C.   AREAS FOR FURTHER RESEARCH

Using the *Liaoning*'s acquisition and development as the basis for the study, this thesis has explored China's employment of deception to conceal its intentions, capabilities and plans. Much of the evidence investigated was directly related to the *Liaoning*'s acquisition and development. There was much indirect evidence concerning carrier-borne aircraft, research and training facilities and military industrial facilities that was insufficiently investigated. Those may yield more evidence that may have an impact on the findings of this thesis.

Chapter VIII's analysis on the future role of the *Liaoning* in the PLAN using Heuer's analysis of competing hypotheses (ACH) proved inconclusive. Continued reassessment of the *Liaoning*'s role should provide a stronger analysis as more evidence becomes available for evaluation. ACH should drive the collection of additional intelligence that could ultimately disprove selected hypotheses.

D.   HOPES FOR THE FUTURE

Interest and concern about China's military capabilities and strategic intentions will continue to increase in the future as the signs point towards continued growth and development in China. The U.S. is ending its major military commitments in Afghanistan and has shifted its emphasis and attention to the Asia-Pacific region after focusing the first decade of the 21st century to on Iraq and Afghanistan. Neither the U.S. nor China would benefit from aggressive strategic rivalry. Both stand to gain from positive strategic co-existence and partnership. However, the cultural and strategic chasm between the two countries is still significant and the case of the *Liaoning* deception illustrates the difference in strategic psyches and perceptions.

The ongoing (2013) tensions between the U.S. and China over cyber-espionage concerns is illustrative. While the U.S. may feel affronted by what it considers as theft from its cyber vaults, China may consider cyber-espionage no more sinister than traditional espionage—everyone does it, no one admits to it and the only rule that matters is not getting caught. It is a struggle for strategic advantage, albeit through the cyber realm. What rules govern behavior between countries at the strategic level when there is no open conflict and diplomatic ties remain cordial? Is China's deceit about its cyber espionage activities very different from its deceit about the *Liaoning*'s acquisition and development? How should the U.S. deal with China over such strategic competition without jeopardizing mutually beneficial relationships and bilateral dialogue? What has the U.S. done to communicate its concerns to China without further complicating the situation? Perhaps to China, the U.S. detailing its alleged cyber espionage activities in the public domain is unnecessary and unhelpful. It restricts China's ability to maneuver and undermines official relations. Just as China does not publicize or even acknowledge the details of its deception regarding the *Liaoning*, it does not publish details about its cyber espionage activities against the U.S because it may regard such activities to be subject to a separate code of behavior to be dealt with outside the usual channels of communications. The U.S. obviously views matters quite differently. Will an improved understanding of China's strategic psyche and modus operandi allow for more effective communication in the future?

As China's naval prowess grows, she will likely build more aircraft carriers. The case of the *Liaoning* provides significant insights into how China employs strategic deception in the development of a significant and visible military capability. Gaining an improved understanding of China's strategic behavior is an important part of Sun Tzu's "knowledge of the enemy." It will allow nation states dealing with China to better deal with her unique strategic behavior and employ the most effective means for engaging her.

This thesis has focused on the "what", "why" and "how" of Chinese strategic deception, using a modern case study to investigate and illustrate the important points of our findings. This thesis does not claim to have deciphered China's *Liaoning* deception definitively but it has attempted to provide an understanding into how China carried out the *Liaoning* deception. Hopefully, this understanding will lead to greater engagement between the U.S. and China in Asia and a healthy respect for each other's strategic customs and traditions. The Middle Kingdom has awakened, but a fight is not the foregone conclusion.

THIS PAGE INTENTIONALLY LEFT BLANK

APPENDIX: THIRTY-SIX STRATAGEMS FROM CHINESE HISTORY

No.	Chinese	Expression	Meaning
	Chapter 1(胜战计) Stratagems employed when in a strategically advantageous posture (绝对优势)		
1	瞒天过海 Mán Tiān Guò Hǎi	Cross the oceans without heaven's knowledge	(1) Those who believe they have taken ample precautions are liable to be caught off guard. (2) Familiarity breeds desensitization and lowers arousal of suspicions.
2	围魏救赵 Wéi Wèi Jiù Zhào	Besiege Wei to save Zhao	Instead of attacking a concentrated enemy, break it up into smaller, vulnerable groups. Bide your time and strike only after the enemy has committed his forces elsewhere.
3	借刀杀人 Jiè Dāo Shā Rén	Murder with a borrowed knife	When enemy intent is clear and allies are hesitant—induce the allies to fight the enemy while preserving oneself.
4	以逸待劳 Yǐ Yì Dài Láo	Wait while the enemy exhausts himself	Lead the enemy into an impasse without fighting or wasting resources. Weaken the active enemy aggressor to strengthen the passive defender.
5	趁火打劫 Chèn Huǒ Dǎ Jié	Loot a burning house	When the enemy suffers a major crisis, seize the chance to gain an advantage.
6	声东击西 Shēng Dōng Jī Xī	Arouse the East but attack the West	Confuse the enemy about your true intentions and strike where his guard is down.
	Chapter 2(敌战计) Stratagems employed when one's strategically posture is equal to the enemy (势均力敌态势)		
7	无中生有 Wú Zhōng Shēng Yǒu	Create something out of nothing	Make a deliberate false move and transform that move into a genuine one after the enemy has been convinced of its falsity.
8	暗渡陈仓 An Dù Chén Cāng	Advance secretly via Chencang	Induce enemy belief in one's original intent while another friendly force flanks the enemy to seize the objective.
9	隔岸观火 Gé An Guān Huǒ	Watch your enemies burn from across the river	When enemy discord is apparent, take no action. Instead, wait for the enemy's oncoming internal upheaval. Internecine struggles cause the enemy to die at its own hand.
10	笑里藏刀 Xiào Lǐ Cáng Dāo	Conceal a dagger behind a smile	Reassure the adversary to cause him to be complacent while working in secret to subdue him. Alternatively, to prepare fully in secret before taking decisive action that does not allow the enemy any opportunity to change his position.

11	李代桃僵 Lǐ Dài Táo Jiāng	Sacrifice the plum to save the peach	Make small tactical sacrifices in order to achieve larger strategic goals.
12	顺手牵羊 Shùn Shǒu Qiān Yáng	Lead away a goat in passing	Take advantage of the smallest flaw to seize the smallest profit. Make use of a minor mistake of the enemy to gain a minor victory.
	Chapter 3 (攻战计) Stratagems employed when in an offensive strategic posture (进攻态势)		
13	打草惊蛇 Dǎ Cǎo Jīng Shé	Beat the grass to frighten the snake out of hiding	Ascertain the doubtful; find out intelligence about the enemy before taking action. Return and bring the enemy's secrets to light.
14	借尸还魂 Jiè Shī Huán Hún	To revive a corpse	Advocates the masterful use of the apparently useless in order to achieve a goal without the adversary's suspicion.
15	调虎离山 Diào Hǔ Lí Shān	Lure the tiger out of the mountain	Avoid attacking the enemy at his position of strength. Plot to entice him into a situation advantageous to you. Also a reminder to reconsider strategy if initial plans fail.
16	欲擒故纵 Yù Qín Gù Zòng	By leaving at large, the better to capture	Pressing the target raises his guard. Leave it unmolested and its guard will lower. Track it but do not press. Fritter away its strength and sap its will. After the target is spent and its guard down, subdue it without undue losses.
17	抛砖引玉 Pāo Zhuān Yǐn Yù	Cast a brick lure to attract jade	(1) Lure the enemy to expend precious resources by the use of counterfeits. (2) Entice the enemy to reveal his motives by making false moves that will arouse his interest.
18	擒贼擒王 Qín Zéi Qín Wáng	To defeat bandits, capture the ringleader	To crush the enemy's main force, capture its leader to decapitate, demoralize and disintegrate the force. The better the leader, the greater the impact of his removal.
	Chapter 4 (混战计) Stratagems employed when in a chaotic strategic posture (军阀混战态势)		
19	釜底抽薪 Fǔ Dǐ Chōu Xīn	Remove firewood from under the cauldron	Avoid a contest of strength with the enemy, instead undermine his position by attacking the fundamental sources of his strength—so that his position will become weaker.
20	混水摸鱼 Hún Shuǐ Mō Yú	Catch a fish in muddled waters	(1) Take advantage of the enemy's internecine fight and exploit its weakness and lack of judgment. (2) Exploit chaos in the enemy's situation or strategic environment.
21	金蝉脱壳Jīn Chán Tuō Qiào	The cicada sloughs its skin	Maintain one's original shape and play out the supposed pose, so that the ally does not doubt and the enemy does not move. Maintaining the appearance of inaction while in fact, taking action in secret.

22	关门捉贼 Guān Mén Zhuō Zéi	Bolt the door to trap the thief	(1) Force a weak enemy into a position of no retreat so that he has nothing to fight for. (2) There is little strategic value in pursuing a defeated enemy at length.
23	远交近攻 Yuǎn Jiāo Jìn Gōng	Forge distant allies and exploit nearby enemies	When circumscribed in situation and restricted in disposition, seek to profit from those nearby and keep peril at a distance.
24	假途伐虢 Jiǎ Tú Miè Guó	Attack via false intentions	For a small state sandwiched between two great powers, if one great power attempts to bring it to submission, the other will impose itself under the pretext of aiding it.

<table>
<tr><td colspan="4" align="center">Chapter 5 (并战计)
Stratagems employed when in a strategically ambiguous posture (友军反为敌态势)</td></tr>
</table>

25	偷梁换柱 Tōu Liáng Huàn Zhù	Steal the beams and swap the pillars	Swap the real with fakes, deceive the enemy into erroneous self-belief about his own strength or one's weakness.
26	指桑骂槐 Zhǐ Sāng Mà Huái	Scolding the Mulberry while criticizing the Pagoda	To channel one's direct criticism at a weaker target (Mulberry plant) while indirectly criticizing the actual stronger target (Pagoda tree). Use indirect methods to achieve one's goals.
27	假痴不癫 Jiǎ Chī Bù Diān	Feign folly even if not insane	Feign foolish ignorance and inaction to hide one's intentions while allowing the enemy to believe you to be foolish and therefore lower his guard.
28	上屋抽梯 Shàng Wu Chou Ti	Upon his reaching the roof, remove his ladder	Provide the enemy with an apparent opportunity to entice it to advance. When it is cut off, trap it in disadvantageous ground to your advantage.
29	树上开花 Shù Shàng Kāi Huā	To make a tree blossom	Exploit external appearances to create an advantageous situation. One can obscure the truth by creating an illusion that the enemy believes in.
30	反客为主 Fǎn Kè Wéi Zhǔ	Reverse the positions of host and guest	To switch strategic posture from passive to active, taking the initiative to the enemy and surprising him.

<table>
<tr><td colspan="4" align="center">Chapter 6 (败战计): Stratagems employed when in a disadvantageous strategic posture
(败军态势)</td></tr>
</table>

31	美人计 Měi Rén Jì	Use beauty to ensnare the opponent	Use ploys to ensnare the enemy by targeting the personal weaknesses of their leader. Once corrupted, discredited and undermined, one's strategic position can be improved.
32	空城计 Kōng Chéng Jì	Empty City stratagem	Use ploys to confuse the enemy's psychology and induce further doubt into his estimations. Typically involves doing what the enemy does not expect one to do.
33	反间计 Fǎn Jiān Jì	Sow distrust in the enemy	Turn the enemy's ploy against him—thus sowing confusion and eroding his strength. Can involve

			foreknowledge of enemy ploy or turning his spies.
34	苦肉计 Kǔ Ròu Jì	Use Self-Inflicted Injury to Beguile the Enemy	Inflict injury upon one's own spy so that he may gain acceptance by the enemy. Capitalize on the known sympathies of the enemy camp to exploit their emotions.
35	连环计 Lián Huán Jì	Use Interlaced Stratagems	Do not engage a stronger enemy head on, instead use stratagems to confuse and weaken him. When stratagems are interlaced, they can produce strategic effects on the enemy and allow the weak to triumph over the strong.
36	走为上计 Zou Wei Shang Ji	When All Else Fails, Retreat is the Best Option	When faced with a superior enemy, one can come to a truce, surrender or retreat. Retreat allows for a counter-attack and can be used to ensnare enemy in pursuit. Retreat is a norm of warfare and does not imply strategic failure.

Sources:

Haichen Sun, *The Wiles of War: 36 Military Strategies From Ancient China* (Beijing: Foreign Languages Press, 1991).

Exploring the Thirty-Six Stratagems (三十六计初探)," *Chinese Strategic Science Network* (中国谋略科学网), http://www.szbf.net/Article_Show.asp?ArticleID=1490

LIST OF REFERENCES

"$1.6b Hotel Plan for Warship." *South China Morning Post*, 11 November 1998.

"2012 World Shipping Statistics." *IHS.* Last accessed 4 June 2013. http://www.ihs.com/products/maritime-information/statistics-forecasts/world-shipbuilding.aspx.

"Admiral Timothy J. Keating." *United States Navy Biography*. Last updated 3 December 2008. http://www.navy.mil/navydata/bios/navybio.asp?bioID=22.

"Aircraft Carriers—CVN." *United States Navy Fact File*. Updated 23 October 2012. http://www.navy.mil/navydata/fact_display.asp?cid=4200&tid=200&ct=4.

"Aircraft Carrier Acquired for Scrap." *South China Morning Post*, 30 August 2000.

"Aircraft carrier competition looms over Asia-Pacific." *The Korean Herald*, 2 November 2007.

Anderson, Eric. C. and Jeffrey G. Engstrom. *China's Use of Perception Management and Strategic Deception*. U.S.-China Economic and Security Review Commission. November 2009. http://www.uscc.gov/Research/china%E2%80%99s-use-perception-management-and-strategic-deception.

Anderson, John Ward. "Turks Keep Ship Going Round in Circles; It's no Longer A Carrier, Not Yet a Casino." *The Washington Post*, 22 July 2001.

Attack on Pearl Harbor 1941: Conclusions of the U.S. Congressional Committee, 1946. London: Stationary Office, 2001.

Axe, David. "China's Testing Woes Remind that Developing Carrier Planes is Hard." *Wired*. 21 March 2013. http://www.wired.com/dangerroom/2013/03/developing-warplanes-is-hard/.

Boorman, Scott A. "Deception in Chinese Strategy" in *The Military and Political Power in China in the 1970s*, edited by William W. Whitson, 313-328. New York: Praeger, 1972.

"Carrier Test Pilot Reveals: High Tempo Training Led Carrier's Arrestor Wire to Fail." Sina News 新浪军事 (China), 18 March 2013. http://mil.news.sina.com.cn/2013-03-18/0859718843.html.

Central Intelligence Agency. "The World Factbook: China." Updated 13 May 2013. https://www.cia.gov/library/publications/the-world-factbook/geos/ch.html.

Chan, Minnie. "Carrier arrives at Qingdao home." *South China Morning Post*, 28 February 2013.

Chan, Minnie. "Carrier could trigger arms race." *South China Morning Post*, 12 January 2009.

Chen, Hu. "Justifiable and reasonable for China to have its own aircraft carriers." *Renmin Ribao*人民日报 (China), 23 April 2009.

Chen, Stephen. "Submarine plants flag on ocean floor." *South China Morning Post*, 30 March 2012. http://www.scmp.com/article/723202/submarine-plants-flag-ocean-floor.

"China continues development of an aircraft carrier." *Jane's Country Risk Daily Report*. 27 May 2009.

"China employs retired Ukrainian admiral." *BBC Summary of World Broadcasts*, 11 March 2003.

"China forms its first carrier aviation unit." People's Daily Online (China), 11 May 2013. http://english.peopledaily.com.cn/90786/8240574.html.

"China launches second aircraft carrier after a £9.6m refit…as a luxury hotel." *Daily Mail (UK)*, 10 August 2011. http://www.dailymail.co.uk/news/article-2024729/China-launches-second-aircraft-carrier-9-6m-refit--luxury-hotel.html?ITO=1490.

"China military officials admit radar lock on Japanese ship." *South China Morning Post*, 18 March 2013. http://www.scmp.com/news/china/article/1193600/china-military-officials-admit-radar-lock-japanese-ship?page=all.

"China not planning to buy aircraft carrier from Ukraine." *Kyodo News Service*, 12 October 1992.

"China Patrols in Asian Seas 'Legitimate': General."*Agence France-Presse*, 2 June 2013. http://www.afp.com/en/news/topstories/chinese-patrols-asian-seas-legitimate-general/.

"China pays S$45m for carrier hull." *The Straits Times* (Singapore), 6 March 2002.

"China plants flag beneath South China Sea." *United Press International,* 26 August 2010. http://www.upi.com/Top_News/US/2010/08/26/China-plants-flag-beneath-South-China-Sea/UPI-27691282870074/.

"China tells more U.S. vessels to keep out." *Central News Network*, 30 November 2007. http://edition.cnn.com/2007/US/11/30/china.us/.

"China to build first aircraft carrier." *Ming Pao*明报 (Hong Kong), 12 January 2000.

"China to produce first aircraft carrier by the year 2000." *Ping Kuo Jih Pao*苹果日报 (Hong Kong), 4 January 1997.

"China's first aircraft carrier commissioned." *Xinhua*, 25 September 2012. http://news.xinhuanet.com/english/china/2012-09/25/c_131871538.htm.

"China's first carrier plans high-sea voyage." *Xinhua* (China), 19 April 2013. http://news.xinhuanet.com/english/china/2013-04/19/c_132323539.htm.

"China's naval ambitions: Congressional report details major warship programmes." *Jane's Navy International*. 20 June 2007.

China's Peaceful Development. Information Office of the State Council of the People's Republic of China. 6 September 2011. http://www.china.org.cn/government/whitepaper/node_7126562.htm.

"Chinese Admiral says China may have aircraft carrier by 2010." *Wen Wei Po*文汇报 (Hong Kong), 7 March 2007.

"Chinese aircraft carrier capability unlikely before 2015, says U.S. report." *Jane's Navy International*. 31 Mar 2009.

"Chinese Businessman Bids £5m for UK's HMS Invincible." *BBC News*, 7 January 2011. http://www.bbc.co.uk/news/uk-12134071.

"Chinese develop special 'Kill Weapon' to destroy U.S. aircraft carriers." *U.S. Naval Institute*. 31 March 2009. http://www.usni.org/news-and-features/chinese-kill-weapon.

"Chinese Military Denies Canadian Media Report which Says that China has Started Building Aircraft Carrier in Shanghai." *Zhongguo Tongxun She* 中国通讯社 (Hong Kong), 28 November 2008.

"Chinese navy repairing unfinished Ukrainian aircraft carrier *Varyag*." *Zhongguo Tongxun She* 中国通讯社 (Hong Kong), 16 August 2005.

"Chinese President attends aircraft carrier 'Liaoning' handover ceremony in Dalian." *Xinhua* (China), 25 September 2012. http://news.xinhuanet.com/english/photo/2012-09/25/c_131872638.htm.

Chuang, Kung-pai. "Chinese Navy Expert refutes 'Aircraft Carrier Threat' Theory."
    Zhongguo Tongxun She 中国通讯社 (Hong Kong), 26 April 2007.

Cole, Bernard D. *The Great Wall at Sea.* Annapolis, Maryland: Naval Institute Press,
    2001.

Collins, Gabe and Andrew S. Erikson. "Implications of China's Military Evacuation of
    Citizens from Libya." Jamestown Foundation: China Brief 11 (4). 10 March 2011.
    http://www.jamestown.org/programs/chinabrief/single/?tx_ttnews%5Btt_news%5
    D=37633&cHash=7278cfd21e6fb19afe8a823c5cf88f07.

Collins, Gabriel and Michael C. Grubb. *A Comprehensive Survey of China's Dynamic
    Shipbuilding Industry.* U.S. Naval War College: China Maritime Studies.
    Newport, Rhode Island: Naval War College Press, 2008.

Daniel, Donald C. and Katherine L. Herbig. *Strategic Military Deception.* New York:
    Pergamon, 1982.

Davenport, Beckman and Tara. "CLCLS submissions and claims to the South China
    Sea." *South China Sea Studies.* Last modified 16 August 2011.
    http://southchinaseastudies.org/en/conferences-and-seminars-/second-
    international-workshop/608-clcs-submissions-and-claims-in-the-south-china-sea-
    by-robert-c-beckman-a-tara-davenport.

Elleman, Bruce A. *Diplomacy and Deception: The Secret History of Sino-Soviet
    Diplomatic Relations, 1917–1927.* Armonk, New Tork: M.E. Sharpe, 1997.

Erickson, Andrew S. and Michael S. Chase. "Informatization and the Chinese People's
    Liberation Army Navy." In *The Chinese Navy: Expanding Capabilities, Evolving
    Roles.* Edited by Phillip C. Saunders, Christopher Yung, Michael Swaine, and
    Andrew Nien-dzu Yang. Washington, DC: Center for the Study of Chinese
    Military Affairs, Institute for National Strategic Studies, National Defense
    University, 2011.

Erickson, Andrew S. and Austin M. Strange, "Learning the Ropes in Blue Water: The
    Chinese Navy's Gulf of Aden Deployments Have Borne Worthwhile Lessons in
    Far-Seas Operations—Lessons that Go Beyond the Antipiracy
    Mission." *Proceedings.* U.S. Naval Institute. 4. April 2013.

Fairbank, John K. *Chinese Ways in Warfare.* Massachusetts: Harvard University Press,
    1974.

Fang, Yang. "President Xi calls for strengthened navy." *Xinhua* (China), 11 April 2013.
    http://news.xinhuanet.com/english/china/2013–04/11/c_132301838.htm.

Fish, Tim. "China's first naval air cadets start training." *Jane's Navy International*. 11 Sep 2008.

Fitzgerald, C.P. *The Chinese View of Their Place in the World*. London: Oxford University Press,1966.

Garnaut, John. "China drops hints about deploying an aircraft carrier." *Sydney Morning Herald*, 24 December 2008.

Godbole, Avinash and Sarabjeet Singh Parmar. *China's Aircraft Carrier: Some Observations*. Institute for Defence Studies and Analyses. 21 April 2011. http://www.idsa.in/idsacomments/ChinasAircraftCarrierSomeObservations_agodbole_210411.

Hai, Tao. "PLA Navy makes preparations for aircraft carrier formation." *Xinhua* (China), 13 December 2012. http://eng.chinamil.com.cn/news-channels/china-military-news/2012-12/13/content_5140986.htm.

Halloran, Richard and Bill Gertz. "China intent on aircraft carrier goal; U.S. commander warns Beijing of challenges." *The Washington Times*, 28 May 2007.

Hardy, James and Poornima Subramaniam. "China Commissions First Aircraft Carrier." *Jane's Navy International*. 25 September 2012.

Hart, B.H. Liddell. *Thoughts on War*. London: Faber and Faber, 1944.

Hastings, Max. *The Korean War*. New York: Simon and Schuster, 1987.

He, Shan. "China aircraft carrier begins 10th sea trial." *China Internet Information Center*, 28 August 2012. http://www.china.org.cn/china/2012-08/28/content_26353139.htm.

Heuer, Richards J. *Psychology of Intelligence Analysis*. Central Intelligence Agency: Centre for Study of Intelligence, 1999.

Heuer, Richards J. "Strategic Deception and Counter-Deception: A Cognitive Process Approach." *International Studies Quarterly* 25, no.2, June 1981, 294-327. Last accessed 3 June 2013. http://www.jstor.org/stable/2600359

"HMAS Melbourne (II)." *Royal Australian Navy*. Last accessed 2 June 2013. http://www.navy.gov.au/hmas-melbourne-ii.

Holmes , James R. and Toshi Yoshihara. *Chinese Naval Strategy in the 21st Century: The Turn to Mahan*. New York: Routledge, 2008.

"Hong Kong paper dismisses report on plan to build aircraft carrier." *Ta Kung Pao* (Hong Kong), 15 January 2000.

Hu, Yinan, Xiaokun Li and Haipei Cui. "Official confirms China building aircraft carrier." *China Daily,* 12 July 2011. http://www.chinadaily.com.cn/china/2011-07/12/content_12881089.htm.

"Is China building a carrier?" *Jane's Defence Weekly.* 11 August 2005.

Jacobs, Andrew. "General hints China's Navy wants to add carrier to fleet." *The New York Times.* 18 November 2008.

Jian Chuan Zhi Shi 舰船知识 (China). No.5, 1987.

Johnston, Alastair Iain. *Cultural Realism.* New Jersey: Princeton University Press, 1994.

Kan, Shirley A. *et al. China-U.S. Aircraft Collision Incident of April 2001: Assessments and Policy Implications.* CRS Report RL30946. Washington , D.C: Library of Congress, Congressional Research Service, 10 October 2001.

"*Kiev* Sale to China 'Will Not Tilt Power Balance." *Straits Times*, 10 May 2000.

Kissinger, Henry. *On China.* New York: The Penguin Press, 2011.

Korean Institute of Military History. *The Korean War.* Volume One. USA: Bison Books, 2000.

Lague, David. "Do China's strategic ambitions include a carrier?" *The International Herald Tribune.* 31 January 2006.

Le Miere, Christian. "Why China sent its aircraft carrier to Qingdao." *International Institute for Strategic Studies*, 7 March 2013. http://www.iiss.org/en/iiss%20voices/blogsections/iiss-voices-2013-1e35/march-2013-6eb6/china-aircraft-carrier-1bb4.

Li, Nan and Christopher Weuve. "China's Aircraft Carrier Ambitions: An Update." *Naval War College Review* 63, no.1 (Winter 2010): 13-31. Last accessed 2 June 2013. http://www.usnwc.edu/getattachment/99679d4b-cbc1-4291-933e-a520ea231565/China-s-Aircraft-Carrier-Ambitions--An-Update.

"*Liaoning*'s role in China's Navy." *South China Morning Post,* 1 October 2012.

Lin, Chong-Pin. "China's Military Modernization: Perceptions, Progress and Prospects." *Security Studies* 3, Issue 4. 1994.

Luo, Guanzhong. *Three Kingdoms*. Abridged edition. Translated by Moss Roberts. New Jersey: University of California Press, 2004.

"Mainland Firm Buys Aircraft Carrier." *South China Morning Post*, 3 September 1998.

Marcus, Jonathan. "China extending military reach." *BBC News Asia-Pacific*, 14 June 2011. http://www.bbc.co.uk/news/world-asia-pacific-13761711.

Melzer, Phillip. "Library of Congress Pinyin Conversion Project: New Chinese Romanization Guidelines." Library of Congress. 3 November 1998. http://www.loc.gov/catdir/pinyin/romcover.html.

Mihalka, Michael. *German Strategic Deception in the 1930s*. RAND Corporation. Santa Monica: RAND, 1980.

"*Minsk* World." Last accessed 2 June 2013. http://www.sz*Minsk*.com/park/.

Moses, Russell Leigh. "Now Sharper, Xi Jinping's 'China Dream' Marks Departure From Past." *Wall Street Journal*, 3 April 2013. http://blogs.wsj.com/chinarealtime/2013/04/03/now-sharper-xi-jinpings-china-dream-marks-departure-from-past/.

"No need to panic about China's aircraft carrier." *Xinhua* (China), 26 September 2012.

Nolton, Brian. "Second Carrier is sent by U.S. as 'precaution': Beijing warns the U.S. on Taiwan Intervention." *New York Times*, 12 March 1996. http://www.nytimes.com/1996/03/12/news/12iht-pent.t.html.

O'Rourke, Ronald. *China Naval Modernization: Implications for U.S. Navy Capabilities —Background and Issues for Congress.* CRS Report RL33153. Washington, DC: Library of Congress, Congressional Research Service, 26 April 2013.

O'Rourke, Ronald. *Navy CVN-21 Aircraft Carrier Program: Background and Issues for Congress.* CRS Report RS20643. Washington, DC: Library of Congress, Congressional Research Service, 25 May 2005.

Office of the Secretary of Defense. *Annual Report to Congress: Military Power of the People's Republic of China 2008.* http://www.defense.gov/pubs/pdfs/China_Military_Report_08.pdf.

Office of the Secretary of Defense, *Annual Report to Congress: Military and Security Developments Involving the People's Republic of China 2012.* May 2012. http://www.defense.gov/pubs/pdfs/2012_cmpr_final.pdf.

Office of the Secretary of Defense. *Annual Report to Congress: Military Power of the People's Republic of China 2013*. Last assessed 4 June 2013. http://www.defense.gov/pubs/2013_china_report_final.pdf

Page, Jeremy. "For Xi, a 'China Dream' of Military Power." *Wall Street Journal*. Eastern edition,13 March 2013.

Paul, Anthony. "The great Chinese aircraft carrier mystery." *The Straits Times* (Singapore), 30 March 2004.

Pedrozo, Raul. "Close Encounters at Sea: The USNS Impeccable Incident." *Naval War College Review* 62, no.3 (Summer 2009).

Perlez, Jane. "Alarm as China issues rules for disputed area." *New York Times*, 1 December 2012. http://www.nytimes.com/2012/12/02/world/asia/alarm-as-china-issues-rules-for-disputed-sea.html?_r=0.

Perlez, Jane. "Dispute flares over energy in South China Sea." *The New York Times*, 4 December 2012. http://www.nytimes.com/2012/12/05/world/asia/china-vietnam-and-india-fight-over-energy-exploration-in-south-china-sea.html?_r=0.

Pilling, David. "Xi Must Show He Can Deliver the 'China Dream.'" *Financial Times*, 25 Apr 2013.

Ramzy, Austin. "China's newest city raises threat of conflict in South China Sea." *Time*, 24 July 2012. http://world.time.com/2012/07/24/chinas-newest-city-raises-threat-of-conflict-in-the-south-china-sea/.

Reed, John. "Is this the prototype for China's first aircraft carrier catapult?" *Foreign Policy*, 28 March 2013. http://killerapps.foreignpolicy.com/posts/2013/03/28/is_this_the_prototype_for_chinas_first_aircraft_carrier_catapult.

Sawyer, Ralph D. *The Tao of Deception*. Cambridge, Massachusetts: Basic Books, 2007.

Schloss, Glenn. "Macau company to convert aircraft carrier into 600m floating palace; $1.6b hotel plan for warship." *South China Morning Post*, 11 November 1998.

Scholss, Glenn and Adam Lee. "Mystery Macau company buys aircraft carrier." *South China Morning Post*, 19 March 1998.

Scobell, Andrew. "Strategic Culture and China: IR Theory versus the Fortune Cookie?" *Strategic Insights* 6, Issue 10. November 2005. Last accessed 3 June 2013. http://hdl.handle.net/10945/11404.

Scott, Richard. "Chinese aircraft carrier capability unlikely before 2015, says U.S. report." *Jane's Navy International*. 31 Mar 2009.

"Secret Chinese report on purchase of Ukrainian aircraft carrier." *Kyodo News Service*, 14 August 1992.

Shi, Naian. *The Water Margin: Outlaws of the Marsh*. Hong Kong: Tuttle Publishing, 2010.

Starr, Barbara. "Chinese Boats harassed U.S. ship, officials say." *Central News Network*, 5 May 2009. http://edition.cnn.com/2009/WORLD/asiapcf/05/05/china.maritime.harassment/index.html.

Starr, Barbara. "Sub collides with sonar array towed by U.S. navy ship." *Central News Network*, 12 June 2009. http://www.cnn.com/2009/US/06/12/china.submarine/.

Storey, Ian. "Soviet carriers find a new home in China." *Jane's Intelligence Review*. 21 March 2002.

Storey, Ian and You Ji. "China's Aircraft Carrier Ambitions: Seeking Truth from Rumors." *Naval War College Review* 57, no.1 (Winter 2004): 77-93. Last accessed 3 June 2013. http://www.usnwc.edu/getattachment/ffc60b3e-d2e6-4142-9b71-6dfa247051f2/

Storey, Ian and You Ji. "Chinese aspirations to acquire aircraft-carrier capability stall." *Jane's Intelligence Review*. 21 March 2002.

Sun, Haichen. *The Wiles of War: 36 Military Strategies From Ancient China*. Beijing: Foreign Languages Press, 1991.

Swaine, Michael D. *China's Maritime Disputes in the East and South China Seas*. 4 April 2013. U.S.-China Economic and Security Review Commission. http://carnegieendowment.org/2013/04/04/maritime-disputes-must-be-carefully-managed/fxea#.

Swaine, Michael D. "Does China Have a Grand Strategy?" *China: Contemporary Political, Economic, and International Affairs*. New York: NYU Press, 2007.

The Diversified Employment of China's Armed Forces. Information Office of the State Council of the People's Republic of China. 16 April 2013. http://www.china.org.cn/government/whitepaper/node_7181425.htm.

Tong, Neng. *Zhong'gong Haijun Xieshi.* (中共海军写实). Beijing: Military Sciences Press, 1999.

"Turkey calls for more guarantees over *Varyag*." *Jane's Defence Weekly*. 14 September 2001.

"Turkey minister to convey message on carrier passage during China visit." *Anatolia News Agency*, 24 August 2001.

"Urgency of building aircraft carriers." *Tangtai* (Hong Kong). No. 26, 15 May 1993.

"U.S. Satellite pictures China aircraft carrier *Varyag*." *BBC News*, 14 December 2011. http://www.bbc.co.uk/news/world-asia-16190926

"Varyag's transformation into an operational aircraft carrier." *The Rising Sea Dragon in Asia*. Accessed 21 May 2013. http://www.jeffhead.com/redseadragon/*Varyag*transform.htm.

Wan, Shuyan. "China's First Aircraft Carrier is Not Intended for Combat Missions." *Zhongguo Xinwen She*中国新文社 (China), 27 July 2011.

Wang, Zheng. "Not Rising, but Rejuvenating: The "Chinese Dream." *The Diplomat*. 5 February 2013. http://thediplomat.com/2013/02/05/chinese-dream-draft/

Whaley, Barton. *Stratagem: Deception and Surprise in War*. Massachusetts: Artech House, 2007.

Yu,Ta-Wei. *Sun Tzu on the Art of War*. Taiwan: Li Ming, 1991.

"三十六计初探"［Exploring the Thirty-Six Stratagems], *中国谋略科学网* [Chinese Strategic Science Network], last accessed 4 June 2013, http://www.szbf.net/Article_Show.asp?ArticleID=1490.